Early religious leaders of Newport; eight addresses delivered before the Newport Historical Society, 1917

Newport Historical Society (Newport, R.I.)

Early Religious Leaders of Newport

Eight Addresses delivered before the Newport Historical Society 1917

☙

Newport, Rhode Island

Published by

The Newport Historical Society

1918

MERCURY PUBLISHING CO.
NEWPORT, R I
1918

PREFACE

The religious element in the history of Newport can never be neglected by one who seeks to obtain a fair impression of the purposes and acts of its first settlers and the events which naturally followed

Driven from the colony of Massachusetts Bay by inability to accept the narrow religious conditions there imposed upon them, the founders of Portsmouth and Newport made welcome to their settlements people of every faith and form of worship, thereby giving what is perhaps the first instance in the history of the world of a free and independent community separating absolutely civil rights from religious opinions

As might be imagined it was but a few years before this invitation was known and accepted; and the little city of Newport soon found among its citizens not only the Baptists and the Congregationalists, the first settlers of the city, but also Friends, Hebrews, Moravian Brethren, the Church of England, and the followers of George Whitefield, who soon organized a Methodist Church.

The history of Newport proves that this broad and liberal policy was wise as well as just These men of different faiths, some of them subject to constant persecution in other colonies, proved themselves most useful, and patriotic, many bringing to the city wealth and a love of literature and of the arts.

CONTENTS

(NOTE—The following papers are arranged in the order, approximately, of the establishment in Newport of the different religious bodies represented)

— ——— - —— —

Dr. JOHN CLARKE

A Paper read before the Newport Historical Society
May 8th, 1917

By
Rev. FRANKLIN G. McKEEVER, D.D.

JOHN CLARKE

Biography is the recounting of the facts of a human life
in their historical relation   Rightly to weigh these facts and
trace their consequences, one must acquaint himself with
their antecedent inspiration, as well as with the history of
events in the midst of which they found expression In this
task the biographer will be influenced and guided by the
known character, inherited or acquired, of the person of
whom he writes

John Clarke was born in Westhorp, Suffolk, England,
October 8, 1609. From his ancestors, through many generations, he must have inherited a love of liberty· for the spirit
of liberty had been long on the wing, seeking for noble souls
of such ample mold as to be able to receive his afflatus. For
more than a century and a half, the thoughtful of Europe
had been awakening from the sleep of ages, until at the beginning of the seventeenth century, tyranny over body or
mind, tenaciously exercised by the strong arm of secular and
ecclesiastical power, was intolerable longer, to men who
claimed the God-given right to think. Such was John
Wycliffe, who on finishing his translation of the Scriptures
into the English tongue, exultantly offered to the plowman
an equal opportunity with the Priest to know the will of God.
Never before had the English people felt such thrills of self-
conscious power and holy ambition to free themselves from
the chains that bound the soul, as when they became acquainted with the dealings of God with ancient nations, and
the incomparable moral ideals of Jesus and his apostles. The
multiplication of printed Bibles following the invention of
movable types by a far-seeing German genius had made this
possible, and set astir not only England but the whole western world like an awakened giant conscious of his powers
The sixteenth century was still young when the Monk of
Wittenberg defied the Holy See, set an example of independence in speech and thought, and proclaimed to all the civil-

ized world a message of personal responsibility to God, and therefore personal freedom from all who interpose themselves between God and the soul. thus laying the corner-stone of a new civilization The Renaissance whetted ambition to a fine edge, and the domination of scholasticism and feudalism, and of the church in secular matters, was over-powered by the onrush of nationalism and humanism Discovery and adventure became a passion. A new heavens and a new earth invited the emancipated spirit of mankind to new prowess. The artist, the philosopher, the scientist, the statesman, the scholar, had his first inspiration to move in the realm of liberty. The great universities became the Mecca of favored sons of fortune, but humbler spirits also claimed the right to think; especially in those spheres which concerned their temporal and eternal well-being—religion and government Encouraged by the benign and brilliant Elizabeth, freedom unfurled a flag never again to be folded while there should be men on earth willing to sacrifice comfort and even life to realize the heaven-born principle of liberty in state and church.

But it must not be supposed that the spirit of freedom had smothered forever the fires of tyranny and persecution James I, succeeded Elizabeth to the throne in 1603. Puritanism had appeared as early as the reign of Edward VI Elizabeth, a Protestant at heart, pursued for state policy, a temporizing course toward the Papacy and disappointed the hopes of her Puritan subjects, extreme Protestants that they were, who boldly taught that the church and state were endowed with separate and distinct functions which were never intended to be united, and that "conscience and not the power of man will drive men to seek the Lord's Kingdom." James I, an extreme reactionist and pronounced bigot, employed his great power to compel all his subjects to respect the Roman doctrine and liturgy, saying of the Puritans: "I will make them conform, or I will harry them out of my kingdom " The record of persecutions and martyrdoms in that reign is a dark blot on the pages of Christian history The most painful sufferers in that period of madness were the Puritans, of whom Macaulay says "The hardy sect grew up and flourished in spite of every thing that seemed likely to stunt it, struck its roots into a barren soil, and spread its branches wide to an inclement sky "

Into this environment came John Clarke Of his progenitors we know little But it is not difficult for the imagination to summon them back to our company from the long past. That they did not lack material possessions; that they prized intellectual and spiritual riches higher than the material, we may justly infer from the record of their illustrious son: "a man of liberal education and of bland and courtly manners." "One of the ablest men of the seventeenth century " "A scholar bred " Unhappily, we have no reliable record as to where John Clarke received his education but facts well substantiated, prove him to have been a man of learning far above the average of his time He is described as a man of high repute for ability and scholarship in languages, including Latin, Greek and Hebrew, law, medicine and theology In his will he bequeathed to a friend, "my Concordance and Lexicon to it belonging, written by myself, being the fruit of several years study, my Hebrew Bibles, Buxtorf's and Pastor's Lexicon, Cotton's Concordance, and all the rest of my books." The Lexicon written by himself, to which reference is here made, is believed to be the one now preserved in the library of Harvard University These, and other literary works assure us that Clarke was a man of learned tastes and attainments Up to the time of his leaving England he was doubtless in sympathy with Puritan views for with them the contemptuously styled Anabaptists of the time held natural affinity, drinking together at the fountain of soul liberty.

John Clarke came to Massachusetts in September, 1637, when that colony was but seven years from its birth. The religious controversy which he found on landing in Boston, seems in the main, trivial to us now But it was such as to induce bitterest strife and kindle the fires of torture and exile, which the state-church was not slow to employ. Anne Hutchinson, keen minded, brave spirited, was the fearless advocate of a free church in a free state. Her followers, among whom were William Coddington, John Clarke, and many other well-to-do and intelligent citizens, were being first disarmed and bereft of protection against the savages,

and then banished from the colony It is not germain to our
subject to enter at length into this not too proud chapter in
our colonial history It has been facetiously said, that the
Puritans on landing in the new world, "first fell on their
knees, and then on the aborigines." Certain it is that the
leaders among the Puritans of John Clarke's day, introduced, or rather imported from the old world, a galling
tyranny, practiced in New England upon others the abuses
that they had come far to escape, and refused to others the
right to differ from them in religious faith and practice. It
was a long time ago. Listening to its recital seems like hearing a lingering echo of the Dark Ages

With the sentence of banishment and torture impend-
ing, the liberty party of Boston resolved to find and found a
new home in the yet untried wilderness, and endeavor to
win the friendship of savage chiefs To the heart of at least
one man of that party, peace was a boon worthy to be cov-
eted and secured even at the cost of protracted hardship
and privation This man was John Clarke He was chosen to
seek out an eligible place for settlement Chilled by the rigors
of a New England winter, and having previously essayed a
more northerly latitude, his party set sail from Boston in the
spring of 1638, with their eyes either on Long Island or the
coast of Delaware But while their vessel was rounding Cape
Cod, Clarke with some companions determined to journey
overland, "to a town called Providence   . which was begun by one M Roger Williams, who for matter of conscience
had not long before been exiled from the former jurisdiction " Williams received the explorers hospitably, and offered valuable suggestions as to two tracts of territory near at
hand · Sowames, now Warwick, and Aquidneck, now Rhode
Island Ascertaining with Williams' aid that the former
lay within the Patent of Plymouth, and resolving, "through
the help of Christ, to get rid of all and be by ourselves," they
investigated the prospect of the latter And finding that
Island unencumbered by English settlers, they, still with the
aid of Mr Williams, set about procuring its possession. In
a fair and friendly way they, in no long time, succeeded in
purchasing Aquidneck on the following terms the payment
of forty fathoms of white beads, to be equally divided be-

tween the two chiefs, Canonicus and Miantonomoh, together with ten coats and twenty hose, to be distributed among the natives on condition that they remove from the Island before the next winter The wily Coddington, of whom we shall have more to say further on, succeeded in having the deed made to him, personally But this action he was later compelled to retract

We may now accompany the adventurers to their newly acquired possession, and see what manner of life they devised for themselves in the new world Here we become acquainted with the invaluable services of John Clarke as a citizen He is now twenty-nine years of age, strong in body, cultivated in mind, and possessed of a well-developed moral sense, to which the liberty of the soul of every man in things pertaining to God, made strong appeal

Before setting out from Boston, eighteen dissenters from the Established Church there—eighteen of the seventy-six who had been disarmed because of suspicion that they might use their weapons in defense against the decrees of the court--formed a compact, which they would use in their new home, as yet "not knowing whither they went.' This agreement reads as follows "We whose names are underwritten, do here solemnly, in the presence of Jehovah, incorporate ourselves into a Bodie Politick, and as He shall help, will submit ourselves, lives and estates, unto our Lord Jesus Christ, the King of Kings and Lord of Lords, and to all those proper and most absolute laws of His given in His holy word of truth; to be guided and judged thereby."

John Clarke's name is the second signature to this compact Passages of Scripture affixed to it turn our thoughts to Clarke as its probable author. These passages are: Exodus 24:3, II Chronicles 11:3,4, II Kings 11 17. The first of these passages bases civil government on divine law The second teaches that religious differences shall not disturb the harmony of the state The third affirms principles long before held by Baptists, that while rendering obedience to the state in civil matters, Christians must be subject, in matters of religion and conscience, only to Christ who is their King and Law-giver

It is not without reason conjectured that the author of

this first compact was John Clarke He was the principal religious teacher of the company. By his advice they were removing from the Massachusetts jurisdiction to enjoy freedom of their consciences, and repeatedly thereafter he taught: "the servant of the Lord must not strive."

When all material affairs relating to the purchase and settlement of Aquidneck had been legally and amicably arranged with the natives, the immigrants from Massachusetts proceeded to establish themselves first on the northern end of the Island, at Pocassett. Evidences of their industry in that locality still exist in wells, etc., there preserved The company proceeded in orderly way to distribute the lands, provide military defence, open highways, collect revenues, hold assemblies, and elect civil officers Breaches of the law of God that tend to civil disturbance came under the jurisdiction of the civil authorities. No religious tests appear in any laws then or thereafter enacted. Liberty in the matter of conscience was accorded to all comers This broad platform attracted large numbers to the Island, and as was to be expected, these additions varied in character as in all new settlements. True however to Puritan instincts, the leaders set up as one of their very first acts, a place of worship The settlement consisted of people of various theological and ecclesiastical persuasions, but all united in worship under John Clarke, a Baptist Elder, (as ministers of that denomination were then called,) as preacher and religious teacher. For, as one remarks, "the mind of John Clarke, balanced, constructive, persuasive, was in the front rank at least, if not foremost of the leaders." It was inevitable that many would follow his teaching and become Baptists. Yet great as was his influence, inherent in the office of the religious minister of that period, rigorous discipline had to be maintained, and the customary penal institutions of the day were found necessary. Breaches of the law were not infrequent, and side by side with the church were set up a prison, a pair of stocks and a whipping post; while fines for offenses that now seem to us puerile were imposed by the magistrate. These, however, were but eddies, incident to the coming of some vicious and troublesome elements into the settlement. The larger part were orderly and valuable citizens

But the whole Island of Aquidneck invited the exploring impulses of the settlers at Pocassett Before a twelvemonth, John Clarke, along with a few companions, had traversed all the shores of the Island, and conceiving its southern end more inviting to permanent plans of a colony, they founded here, in the spring of 1639, a settlement which they called Newport, having first rechristened their whole purchase, "the Isle of Rhodes," from the Island of that name in the Mediterranean Sea. Before another year had passed there were found to be about two hundred families in the Newport settlement. John Clarke, with two assistants, had been commissioned to survey and apportion the lands to a distance of five miles, and all the arrangements of an orderly government had been instituted Not the least of these was the provision for religious worship. Religious toleration prevailed, spite of denominational differences There were, amongst the settlers, Baptists from England, members of John Cotton's church in Boston who had adopted Baptist sentiments, and others in a state of transition. To the whole of this heterogeneous population Dr. Clarke ministered in religious things. We do not read of serious disagreement as to their beliefs for many years, and there appears to have been no neglect of social worship. A despised and persecuted sect both in England and in the Massachusetts Bay Colony, the Baptists of Rhode Island exhibited a tolerant and catholic spirit in their new home, and the settlers showed their appreciation of it by accepting John Clarke both as civil and religious leader. Amongst his hearers on the Sabbath were, without doubt, William Coddington, first elected judge, Anne Hutchinson, the reformer, two brothers of the minister, and not a few others whose names are perpetuated in the honored families of the Island to this day.

At exactly what date a church was instituted, avowing the principles and using the practice of Baptists, we do not know, for the early records are not preserved. "But," as an historian of the First Baptist Church of Newport remarks, "while the date of its origin is veiled in obscurity, there is no uncertainty as to its first minister," a position which Dr. Clarke adorned to the close of his life.

While thus engaged, and also practicing his profession

as a physician, this Christian minister was the inspirer and organizer of most if not all the advance movements in civic affairs. He not only occupied at different times, responsible offices under the government, but he is with good reason supposed to be the potential author of the government itself. The first aggressive move for a charter for the Island of Aquidneck and adjacent Islands and lands was made in 1642, when a committee of whom John Clarke was a member was appointed to draw up a petition to Parliament, and at the same time to seek the assistance of Sir Henry Vane, then influential at court Previous to this, endeavors to the same end had been made by Clarke himself, almost unaided. When five years later, 1647, Rhode Island became a State under a charter accredited by many to the efforts of Roger Williams, its provisions and code of laws are declared by Williams himself, to be modeled after those in force in Newport It is supposed, and for good reasons, that John Clarke was the author of the government framed: both of the code of laws and of the means of enforcing it. That code concludes with these words. "And otherwise than thus what is herein forbidden, all men may walk as their consciences persuade them, every one in the name of his God And let the saints of the Most High walk in this colony without molestation, in the name of Jehovah their God, forever and ever "

While Dr Clarke was thus busy with weighty affairs of state, we find him engaged in tasks which he must have regarded as of quite equal moment. Now he is in Providence, endeavoring to resusitate churches otherwise uncared for, and again, making fatiguing journeys to minister to small groups of believers, who, not finding churches of their faith within easy reach had continued their membership with the church at Newport. Such was one William Witter, aged, blind and infirm, living near the then village of Lynn, Massachusetts. In July, 1651, he entreated his pastor to visit him and administer spiritual consolation Taking with him Obediah Holmes and John Crandall, elders connected with the church in Newport, Dr. Clarke essayed the no inconsiderable journey The three reached Witter's home in the evening of Saturday, and while engaged in administering the duties of their office on the Sabbath, they were arrested on a warrant issued by the magistrate, and later presented before the court in Boston. The charges preferred against the strangers were concerned with teachings contrary to those of the standing, ecclesiastical order. Clarke proposed to discuss publicly their differences, but he was summarily and rudely denied that privilege "Without producing either accuser, witness, jury, law of God or man," Governor John Endicott pronounced sentence as follows: that John Clarke should pay a fine of twenty pounds or else be well whipped, that Obediah Holmes should pay a fine of thirty pounds or else be well whipped, and John Crandall should pay a fine of twenty pounds or else be well whipped. Holmes refused to acknowledge himself a criminal by either paying his fine or permitting any one to pay it for him. "I durst not accept deliverence in such way," he said. The record of how he was "unmercifully whipped" on a September day in Boston, two magistrates being present to see it done severely; how, for taking Holmes by the hand after his punishment, two spectators were apprehended, imprisoned, and sentenced to pay a fine of forty shillings or be whipped, is one of the shame-spots in Puritan colonial history Kind friends paid the fines of Clarke and Crandall without their consent, and the latter was at once released, but Clarke was held in custody for some time afterward when he also was released "to be gone out of the colony"

On his return to Newport, Dr. Clarke found the colony in peril, and its government in jeopardy William Coddington was president of the four united towns in 1648. and continued in that office until the execution of Charles I, in 1649 In the midst of the confusion incident to the accession of the Commonwealth, this astute politician sailed secretly to England, and succeeded in obtaining a commission as governor for life, of the Islands of Aquidneck and Conanicut, thus nullifying the charter of 1643. The whole colony was moved to a high degree of indignation, and in 1651, the two men most able and most representative of the people, John Clarke for the Rhode Island towns, and Roger Williams for the towns of Warwick and Providence Plantations, were despatched to England to secure the withdrawal of Coddington's commission. Their mission accomplished, Williams returned to Providence in 1654, and Clarke remained at court as guardian of the interests of the reunited Commonwealth at home.

And then began an epoch in this great man's life, which, for diplomatic efficiency and self-sacrificing devotion, has seldom been equaled in the annals of public service. Dr. Clarke remained in England twelve years, nearly the whole of the time at his own charges; for the meager appropriation of two hundred pounds, voted by the colony, was not collected till long after, and then only when a further vote prohibited the payment of any bills until this debt, increased to three hundred and forty-three pounds seventeen shillings, was paid Meantime Clarke was obliged to mortgage his property at home. During the whole period he was engaged in literary and ministerial labors to eke out his living, while employed specifically, in service for the state. Yet his life at this time could not have been wholly without compensation, since two of his intimate friends and helpers of his plans were Sir Henry Vane and John Milton

The year after reaching England, or in 1652, Dr. Clarke published a book entitled· "Ill Newes from New England or a Narrative of New England's Persecutions." In this volume it is declared that "while old England is becoming new, New England is becoming old." And in this volume he incorporated the substance of a tract previously written, entitled "A Brief Discourse Touching New England, and Particularly Rhode Island, as also a Faithful Relation of the Prosecution of Obediah Holmes, John Crandall and John Clarke, merely for Conscience Toward God, by the Principle Members of the Church or Commonwealth of Massachusetts, in New England, which Rules Over that Part of the World"

The years passed on and Clarke successfully parried the determined efforts of the agents of the other colonies to thwart the far reaching purposes of Rhode Island to foster and maintain a government hospitable to religious liberty On the death of Cromwell, and the accession of Charles II, in 1660, the labor of years would probably have come to naught but for the able diplomacy of John Clarke. A new charter was an imperative necessity, if Rhode Island's rights and liberties were to be preserved To this task Dr Clarke unreservedly addressed himself He appealed by letters to the King, in which he professed the loyalty of the colony to the Crown, and argued for the granting of a charter of civil corporation His constituents would establish a corporate government duly protected by English law, so far forth as the nature and constitution of the place and the professed cause of their consciences would permit. "Your petitioners have it much on their hearts," he says, "to hold forth a lively experiment that a flourishing Civil State may stand, yea, and best be maintained, and that among English spirits, with a full liberty in religious concernments, and that true piety, rightly grounded upon Gospel principles, will give the best and greatest security to true sovereignty, and will lay in the hearts of men the strongest obligations to truer loyalty."

It is no small tribute to the greatness of Dr Clarke's diplomatic skill that, spite of the determined opposition in Parliament, and the no less determined opposition from Massachusetts and Connecticut, he, on the eighth day of July 1663, obtained the signature and seal of that astute Monarch, Charles II. It is noteworthy that freedom of worship and of conscience was made the basis of individual rights And considering the times, it is amazing that such a provision as the following could emanate from the English throne "Our royal will and pleasure is, that no person within the said colony, at any time hereafter, shall be anywise molested, punished, disquieted, or called in question, for any differences of opinion in matters of religion " Not without reason is Dr. Clarke believed by many, including Thomas Jefferson, to have been the author of this epoch-making document, which became the constitutional law of Rhode Island and Providence Plantations from the time of its enactment until the American revolution, and whose provisions Jefferson incorporated into the constitution of the new republic

His arduous task accomplished Dr. Clarke turned his face again toward Newport and his family, from whom he had been separated twelve years, and was received with marked demonstrations of honor and gratitude At a public meeting of the citizens, November 24, 1663, the charter was read, the stamp and seal of his Majesty, Charles II, were duly displayed, and thanks were voted to the King, to the Earl of Clarendon, who had been the friend and helper of the enterprise, and to John Clarke It was Newport's day.

Dr. Clarke had now given twenty-five years to public service for the colony which he founded. He had fostered religion and education, having at the very beginning of the settlement instituted a public school, the first in America if not in the world, and a Church, which, after two hundred and seventy-eight years is still in existence and at the present time bears his name. One would expect to find him, at the age of fifty-five, wishing to devote his remaining years to those beloved interests, along with the practice of his profession as a physician. But the colony was not yet ready to dispense with his services and counsel He was elected to various public offices, was appointed by the first Assembly under the charter, to revise and codify the laws, and was for three successive years elected Deputy Governor, two of those years serving in that office.

But time, for this man of many parts, was hastening, and dear to him as life was the Kingdom of God. As he entered upon what was to be the last decade of human existence, his mind turned affectionately toward that object, and his remaining energies and matured judgment were placed more fully at its service. Five years before his death he retired from all public office; but that did not exempt him, only sixteen days before the final summons from the Ruler of All, from a summons from the General Assembly. "the Assembly desiring to have the advice and concurrence of the most judicious inhabitants in the troublous times and straits into which the colony has been brought." Seven days later he was put in charge of the Island's defenses.

Dr Clarke died suddenly April 20, 1676. His ashes lie in an unkempt cemetery, the land of which was once owned by himself, on West Broadway, in Newport. His grave is a perpetual reminder of the ingratitude of republics He bequeathed his estate to a self-perpetuating body of trustees, to be forever devoted to the causes of religion and education, in the Church and city which he founded, the poor being the special objects of his beneficence Thus "he being dead yet speaketh "

The theological beliefs of Dr Clarke were those held throughout their history by the body of Baptists, and his doctrinal writings, the fruit of his profound studies of later years, are in accord with Baptist Confessions of Faith From the same fountain he also drank in those principles concerning magistracy and religious liberty, so dominant in his life, and which became the warp and woof of the charter of 1663 It was the guiding hand of John Clarke that steered the ship of our state clear of the rocks that split both England and Massachusetts asunder. "His is the glory of first showing in an actual government, that the best safeguard of personal rights is Christian law, that church and state may safely be separated, and that absolute license of thought and utterance not issuing in crime against persons and estates, may be most rightly and wisely placed far above toleration, on the secure basis of personal statute "

History bears undivided testimony to John Clarke's claim to the veneration and gratitude, not alone of Rhode Island, but of all mankind A successor of his in the pastorate, Rev. John Callender, who lived among men who knew Dr Clarke, wrote "To no man is Rhode Island more indebted than to him No character in New England is of purer fame than is John Clarke." Isaac Backus, the Baptist historian of the eighteenth century, said of him "Mr. Clarke left as spotless a character as any man I know of that ever acted in any public station in this country.   . I have not met with a single reflection cast upon him by any one." Governor Arnold's opinion was "His character and talents appear more exalted the more closely they are examined."

    "One of the ablest men of the seventeenth century He was a ripe scholar, learned in the practice of two professions, besides having large experience in diplomatic and political life With all these public pursuits, he continued the practice of his original profession as a physician, and also retained the pastoral charge of his church. His life was devoted to the good of others He was a patriot, a scholar, and a Christian. The purity of his character is conspicuous in many trying scenes, and his blameless, self-sacrificing life disarmed detraction. and left him without an enemy." Let one more testimonial from history suffice George Bancroft says: "Never did a young Commonwealth possess a more faithful friend The modest and virtuous Clarke, the persevering and disinterested envoy,   . whose whole life was a continual exercise of benevolence. Others have sought office to advance their fortunes. He parted with his little means for the public good He had powerful enemies in Massachusetts, and left a name without a spot."

The last act of this scholar, physician, minister, statesman, patriot, was worthy of his pious and philanthropic spirit His will, signed on the day of his death, "willingly and readily" commits his soul into the hands of his "merciful Redeemer;" provides that his body be "decently interred, without any vain ostentation;" and that his estate be administered for "the bringing up of children unto learning," civil and religious, and for the relief of the poor.

Efforts more or less spasmodic and inadequate have been made in recent years to honor the name and perpetuate the memory of Dr Clarke, but as has been before pointed out, the duty belongs not alone to Newport, nor to Rhode Island, but to our whole nation, which bears the honor through him, of possessing the first government on earth which gave to all equal civil and religious liberty

The Early History of the Friends in Newport

A Paper read before the Newport Historical Society
August 14th, 1917

By

WILLIAM I. HULL

Professor of History in Swarthmore College

The Religious Society of Friends

I fear that it may seem very much like "carrying coal to Newcastle" for me, a Baltimorean by birth and a Pennsylvanian by adoption, to present to an audience of Newport historical students a discourse on what must be to them so familiar a theme as the one assigned me. But perhaps a lack of new information may be atoned for by a sympathetic appreciation of the opportunity afforded to the Friends in Rhode Island to practise without interference or molestation the faith and ideals which inspired them It may well be that a Maryland and Pennsylvania Quaker, familiar with the religious toleration granted in their respective colonies by Lord Baltimore and William Penn, can doubly appreciate the religious liberty established by Roger Williams, William Coddington, and their compeers in Rhode Island.

It may be permitted me to plead, also, that my interest in the early Friends of Newport has a personal as well as a religious origin. For, coming to the neighboring island of Conanicut a score of years ago for the first of a series of summer sojourns, I was pleased to find here one link in my own family chain which has stretched from Massachusetts and Maine, through Rhode Island, Connecticut and New York, down to Maryland. Captain John Hull of Newport and Conanicut was the third link in that chain and my children are the tenth. Across the gulf of two centuries and a half he speaks to his descendants; and as one of the early Friends of Newport, and a type, doubtless, of many, he may engage our attention for a few moments. The grandson of Rev. Joseph Hull, who settled a colony of 106 persons in Weymouth, Massachusetts, in 1636, and the son of Tristram, the first of the family to embrace Quakerism, John was born in Barnstable and adopted his father's religious faith and his occupation of captain in the merchant marine Many of the Quaker emigrants to Pennsylvania were brought over in John Hull's ships, during the great exodus in the Eighties under William Penn; but he sailed for the most part between Newport and London In the lattter city he became acquainted with and married a young Quakeress, Alice Tiddeman, by name. and three years afterwards, in 1681, came with his wife and infant daughter Mary to Newport Thirty years' before this, William Coddington. Benedict Arnold and three associates had purchased the Island of Conanicut. and here John Hull bought a farm of 370 acres and in 1690 built a house upon it and settled his family in it His fifth child and second son, John, who was also my ancestor, was born in this house and is said by your local historians to have been the first white child born upon the island

With Indian neighbors and other Friends' families who settled gradually upon the island, John lived in the intervals of his sea-faring life, and to his Conanicut home he retired in old age, dying there an octogenarian about the year 1732. His house was burned by the British during the Revolution, but his farm is still called the "Old Hull Place;" and nearby is a thicket called "Hull's Swamp," where the patriots concealed themselves and their valuables during the Revolution and thus incited the British to cut down the fine old trees and burn the bushes

John Hull's farm evidently made quite a landsman of him, for we learn from the records that he served Jamestown for a score of years as asssessor, town-clerk, head-warden, town councillor, and representative for a half-dozen terms in the colonial legislature But the chroniclers of Newport have been chiefly interested in his career as a sea-captain and especially his connection with Admiral Sir Charles Wager, afterwards first Lord of the British Admiralty, and appointed Privy Councillor by Queen Anne. Wager's maternal grandfather was Admiral Wilham Goodson, and his father was Admiral Charles Wager, while he was closely related to Admiral Sir Thomas Tiddeman.* Of his father, the diarist Pepys records: "There was never any man that behaved himself in the Straits [of Gibralter] like poor Charles Wager, whom the very Moors do mention with tears some-

---

*The names Wager and Tiddeman have been borne by sundry members of the Hull family.

times " Of Wager himself, the historian Walpole says "Old Charles Wager is dead at last and has left the fairest character." The younger Charles died in 1743, aged seventy-nine, and was buried in Westminster Abbey.

> "He lies where the minister's groined
> arches curve down
> To the tomb-crowded transept of
> England's renown "

The remains of his preceptor lie in an unmarked grave, —is it in the Coddington Grave-yard in Newport, or in some over-grown and forgotten God's acre on Conanicut? The story of his life is recorded in England's naval history and the lovers of lighter literature may find some of its incidents. in considerably distorted form, in Colonel Joseph C Hart's novel, "Miriam Coffin "* Here it is mentioned simply for the sake of associating him with the early Friends of Newport, and it may not be inappropriate to rehearse its best known incident which illustrates both his own character and that of John Hull, from whom his seamanship was learned His father died when Charles was an infant, and his mother married a London merchant and Friend. Alexander Parker. The call of the sea was loud in the London boy's heart, and he was apprenticed in youth to Captain John Hull, his parents' friend John, who was about a dozen years his senior. is said to have remarked to him when he appeared at his ship· "Step on board, Charles: perhaps thou may get to be a captain one of these days." And the youth, with his father's example in mind, replied "I shall be disappointed if I do not get to be an admiral " An English merchant ship was often attacked by French and Spanish privateersmen in those days of Louis XIV's aggressive warfare, and John Hull's Quaker ship was not immune from such attacks On one of these occasions, the story goes, a French armed schooner bore down upon him in the British Channel, and at Wager's urgent request John retired to the cabin and Wager was left in charge of the ship to deal with the privateersman It appears, however, that Wager's manoeuvers did

---

*The first edition of this story was published in San Francisco, in 1834 ; the 2nd. edition, in the same city, in 1872

not commend themselves to Captain Hull, who called out to
him from the companion-way "Charles, if thou intend to
run over that schooner, thou must put the helm a little more
to the starboard" Charles followed the advice and sank the
schooner with all on board. Captain Hull, we are glad to be
informed, after this lapse from his Quaker principles, got his
ship about as soon as possible to rescue the privateersman's
crew but a stiff breeze and heavy sea prevented the finding
or rescue of a single victim * When the ship arrived in London and the story was told, the Admiralty warmly com-
mended Hull and offered him a captaincy in the royal navy.
In moments free from excitement and professional pride,
however, John was too much of a Quaker to accept such an
offer; but he yielded to his apprentice's desire and recommended him to the Admiralty, from whom came an ap-
pointment as midshipman Wager rose to the admiral's rank
in the British navy, and never became a Friend; but he seems
to have cherished always an admiration and gratitude for
his Quaker instructor, "my honored master," as he called
him, sending him yearly a pipe of wine, and visiting him
often in Newport and Conanicut. †

Long before John Hull settled in Newport, however, the
Friends had made it their home In fact, before the first
Quakers from England found their way thither, it was the
home of a group of people who appear to have been Quakers
in all but name The followers of Anne Hutchinson and of
Samuel Gorton, who found a refuge in Rhode Island from
their Massachusetts persecutors, had some striking points
of resemblance with their later contemporaries, the Quakers, and some of them joined the Society of Friends when it
established its meetings among them a score of years later

---

*Connected with this, or another similar occasion, there is another story
(which was told me by your late distinguished townsman, Honorable Wm.
P Sheffield, but which it may be permitted a descendant to hope is apocry-
phal), that when John Hull, looking out of a porthole saw a Frenchman lay
hold of a rope with the intent of climbing on board, he quietly cut the rope,
saying to him "Friend, if thee wants that rope, thee may have it "

†One branch of the family of Hull still remains on Conanicut Island, and
for many years after John's death his descendants retained membership in
the Society of Friends and were prominent in the religious and political life
of the island and of Newport.

But there was another group of the founders of Rhode Island who still more closely resembled the Friends in doctrine and practice, and who also later joined the society. These were among the founders of Portsmouth and Newport, with William Coddington and Nicholas Easton at their head. They were "antinomians," like the Hutchinsonians and Gortonians, and like them were driven from Massachusetts to their refuge on Aquidneck, or Rhode Island proper. Here, religious differences caused them to separate from their fellow-exiles in Portsmouth, in 1638, and the next year to leave Portsmouth and found Newport. Their leader in Massachusetts, Portsmouth and Newport was William Coddington, who was elected the first "judge" in Portsmouth and Newport as well. When the two settlements united, in 1640, Coddington was elected the new colony's first governor, and under his leadership the people in popular assembly declared, in May, 1641, for the two great American and Quaker principles of self government and religious liberty. "It is ordered," runs one of the famous resolutions, "that none bee accounted a delinquent for doctrine."[*]

Where there is liberty, there is always diversity, and in Newport there developed as early as 1641 two main groups of religious thinkers, one, under the leadership of John Clarke, which united with the Baptists, and one, under Coddington's leadership, which formed a kind of Quaker meeting. Thus, nearly a score of years before the real Quakers came to Newport, and a half-dozen years before the Founder of Quakerism began his public mission in England, Newport saw the rise of what might be called a Pre-Foxian, Quaker people. They looked askance upon a separate, exclusive clergy; laid great stress on spirituality in ministry and worship, sought for this spirituality in the Divinity that doth dwell within man himself; and were adverse to relying upon "carnal" as opposed to "spiritual weapons." As illustrative of this last principle, they cooperated with Roger Williams the Baptist and set an example for William Penn the Quaker

---

[*]The author desires to acknowledge here his indebtedness for many details in this paper to Professor Rufus M Jones's very readable book, " The Quakers in the American Colonies," N Y , 1911, and also to your Society's admirable collection of books and manuscripts

in a just and peaceful dealing with their Indian neighbors, and at least one of their number, Nicholas Easton, was fined five shillings in 1639 for refusing to carry weapons to meeting *

New England, like Old England, was seething during these years with many varieties of extreme Puritans, and Rhode Island had more than its share, thanks to its religious tolerance, of these varied seekers after God. Massachusetts did its best to curb or expel them, and regarded Rhode Island as a horrible example of the folly of toleration. Cotton Mather called it "the Gerizzim of New England" and wrote: "I believe there never was held such a variety of religions together on as small a spot of ground as have been in that colony." If a man should lose his religion, he suggests, he might find it there "at the general muster of the opinionists."

It is small wonder, then, that the Quakers should have found congenial soil, with seed already sown, in Newport, and that the town should have become both a nursery of Quakerism and a place whence it was transplanted to other parts of New England.

The chief reasons why the Quakers were persecuted by the Puritans of Boston were precisely the reasons why they found toleration and prosperity in Newport These were, first, the Puritans' fear of the Dutch, the French, and the Indians, and it is notorious that fear hath no ears; but the Rhode Islanders placed all their dealings with these possible foes on a basis of justice and friendship, hence feared them not, and were not obliged to seek strength abroad through suppression and enforced uniformity at home. Again, the Puritan clergy were chiefly responsible for persecution in New England, while the democratic laity were opposed to it, —as was shown especially in the case of the Gortonites and the Quakers; but in Rhode Island there was no established clergy to act as guardians over the state or to inflame the persecution of dissenters Again, the Puritans feared and detested the doctrine of private inspiration and denounced its exponents, like Anne Hutchinson and Samuel Gorton, as "proud and pestilent seducers;' but in Rhode Island this doctrine was like a native element and seemed to its popu-

*Rhode Island Colonial Records, I 95.

lation of "Seekers" as natural as the sunshine. Finally, the Puritan union of church and state, the separation of the clergy from the laity, the primacy of the clergy in secular affairs, the collection of tithes, were all threatened by the Quakers' denial of their right to exist: but Rhode Island had acted from the beginning on the American principle of entire separation between church and state, and hence charged not this against the Quakers as a heresy and a mence to the public weal or safety.

While it is easy to explain the reasons for religious persecution elsewhere in New England and its absence in Rhode Island, the fact remains as the corner-stone of Rhode Island's history, and the student of its history in full appreciation of this fact might almost wish that the emblem upon its shield should be not even Hope or Faith, but Charity, which is greatest of the things that endure. Newport not only accorded toleration to the Quakers, but, as has been stated, it paved the way for them by developing a home-made Quakerism of its own. The leader of this group of Quaker aborigines was the pioneer and founder of the settlement as well, William Coddington. Our friends the Baptists lay just claim to Roger Williams, the founder of Providence; but as "there is glory enough to go round" they may well yield first place in Rhode Island proper to William Coddington. John Clarke, it is true, was in the front rank of Rhode Island's founders. and he appears to have founded the first Baptist church in America. It would be unseemly to repeat, in behalf of the two leaders and the two rival communities in the early settlement, the slogan of "Coding's your friend, not Short!"; but in the interest of historic truth it may be recalled that Coddington was one of the founders of Massachusetts; that he was active in the affairs of that colony even before Boston was named, that he built Boston's first house, which became the Governor's house for many years,—including those during which the governors persecuted Coddington's fellow-Quakers, that he secured in 1637 the deed from Canonicus and Miantonomo, the two chief sachems of the Narragansetts, which conveyed the Island of Aquidneck, or Rhode Island, to "William Coddington and his friends;" that he held the island in his own name for fifteen years and then transferred all rights which he might claim under the deed to the company of which he was the leader; that in 1638, when Portsmouth was settled and a compact for civil government was signed by the settlers, Coddington's name was first among the signatures and Clarke's came second; that in 1639, when it was agreed to settle Newport, Coddington was the first of the nine pioneers who signed the agreement, that he was the first ' judge" in Portsmouth and the first in Newport, the first governor of the two settlements united (1640-1647), the President of the united colony of Rhode Island and Providence in 1648, and commissioned proprietor of the Narragansett Islands and governor for life of both Rhode Island and Connecticut in 1651. This last position was resented by his fellow-Rhode Islanders and he was alienated from them for a time;* but he manfully withdrew his claims within a year and was at once elected by Newport to the General Court. When in 1663 a charter was granted to the united colony of Providence and Rhode Island, its four leading citizens, Arnold, Brenton, Coddington, and Easton, were mentioned in alphabetical order, and the other incorporators regardless of order

At the age of seventy-four, Coddington was elected governor for two terms (1674-6) and in that office presided over Rhode Island's destiny during King Philip's terrible war. While governor of Aquidneck in 1640, he had made a treaty of friendship with the Narragansett Indians, and thus set an example for his great Quaker successor in Pennsylvania forty-two years later. But unlike Penn, he lived to see his colony ravaged by Indian foes. He and his fellow-Quakers did their best to prevent the war, and then to shield the mainland of Rhode Island from its horrors. Pessicus, the chief of the Narragansetts, was very kindly disposed towards the colony and its Quaker rulers, but told them that he could restrain his chieftains on the island alone, but not on the mainland. Thus, while the mainland was devastated, the island became, in the words of the old chronicler, Drake, "the common Zoar, or place of refuge for

---

*The trouble came to a head in 1648, and seems to have been due in the first place to Coddington's determination that Rhode Island should not enter the New England Confederation

the distressed." As Holland has been to the Belgian refugees of our day, so Newport and her sister towns on the island became the hosts and guardians of the many fugitives who fled from the Indian tomahawk and fire-brand. The assembly appointed a committee of six, including three Quakers (Walter Clarke, Joshua Coggeshall and Caleb Carr), to urge the mainland inhabitants to come to the island, to supply each fugitive family with land, or with a cow to be pastured on the commons, and to distribute £800 for their support.

At this time, too, the Quakers of Newport had a golden opportunity of heaping coals of fire upon the heads of their Massachusetts persecutors In the winter of 1675-76, after the battle at South Kingstown, the wounded New England soldiers were brought to Newport by the Quakers and cared for in their homes. The Massachusetts and Confederation authorities expressed their thanks for this kindness; but when they made the further request that Rhode Island should send 100 or 200 soldiers to the trenches, as well as provide Red Cross aid, Governor Coddington replied with a Quaker refusal to fight, and reminded the Massachusetts petitioners that at that very time the Massachusetts clergy were lamenting, as one of the sins which had caused the war, "the recent neglect to suppress the Quakers and their meetings " and the Massachusetts authorities were enforcing a fine of £5 and imprisonment at hard labor on bread and water for any person who should attend a Quaker meeting!

At the time of the Revolution, also, Massachusetts was feign to accept the charity of the Rhode Island Quakers. A committee of them took £1968 to distribute among the victims of the siege of Boston, and in company with the selectmen they went from house to house distributing food, clothing and fuel. These activities were pursued in sixteen Massachusetts towns, through many of which the Quakers had been whipped at the cart-tail a century before. Salem, and probably other towns, made an *amende honorable* by passing votes of thanks to the Quaker philanthropists in 1775 and 1776.

After King Philip's war, Massachusetts denounced the Quaker war-policy of Rhode Island as "scarcely showing English spirit;" and within the colony itself there was a strong militant opposition, which succeeded in replacing the Quaker governor, Walter Clarke, by the chief Quaker rival and twelve-times governor, Benedict Arnold But Arnold died before his term was ended, and Coddington was again elected to the governor's chair. By this time, however, he was in his seventy-eighth year and worn out by the many heavy labors and strange vicissitudes of his life, and he too died before his term of office expired.

The verdict of two of Rhode Island's historians upon this pioneer Rhode Islander and pioneer Quaker in Newport gives some idea of his strength and his weakness. Callender says of him. "A good man, full of days. he died promoting the welfare and the prosperity of the little commonwealth which he had in a manner founded." And Judge Durfee hands down as his opinion that "he had in him a little too much of the future for Massachusetts and a little too much of the past for Rhode Island,"—which opinion emphasizes, perhaps, the defects of Massachusetts and the merits of Rhode Island, rather than those of Coddington A student of physiognomy as well as of history may be able to strike the balance between these and other conflicting opinions of him by a study of his portrait which hangs in Newport's city hall *

The citizens of Newport erected a monument in his memory on the two hundredth anniversary of the town's settlement, and inscribed upon it this tribute:

> That illustrious man, who first purchased this Island from the Narragansett Sachems Conanicus and Miantonomo for, and on account of himself and Seventeen others his associates in the purchase and Settlement
>
> He presided many years as chief Magistrate of the Island and Colony of Rhode Island and Died much respected and lamented on the 1st. day of November, 1678 Aged 77 years.

He was buried, the old records say, on the "6 day of ye 9 mo. 1678;" and around him in death as in life, in the Coddington Burial-ground which is located appropriately on

---

*A copy of this portrait is in the Redwood Library , but there are good reasons for believing that this portrait is not authentic Cf the Bulletin of the Newport Historical Society No 9 (October, 1913): "On the So-called Portrait of Governor William Coddington in the City Hall at Newport," by Hamilton B. Tompkins

Farewell St., there lie the remains of a number of his associates and their descendants His own son, William Coddington, Jr., who was governor from 1683 to 1685, and died at the age of thirty-seven; sundry members of the Thurston, Martin, James and Wanton families, and doubtless many another "rude forefather of the hamlet sleeps, Each in his narrow cell forever laid," but left in Quaker oblivion and not marked by visible sign

One of the village Hampdens whose graves are marked is Nicholas Easton, who died August 15, 1675, at the age of eighty-three. He was a pioneer in Newbury, Massachusetts, and built the first Englishman's house in Hampton. Coming to Rhode Island for religion's sake, he was one of the nineteen signers of the Portsmouth "contract," and the second signer of the Newport "Agreement" With his two sons, Peter and John, he rowed down from Pocasset (Portsmouth) to an island in Newport's harbor, which he called Coaster's Harbor, now the site of the Naval War College and Training School, and which may be regarded as being, historically, to Newport what Cape Cod is to Plymouth The Eastons built the first house and the first wind-mill in Newport, on Marlborough St.; but the house was destroyed by fire in 1641, and a modern jail stands on or near the site of the mill.

Easton became a Friend, with Coddington and most of his other associates, about 1657, but remained one of the pillars of the state as well as of the Quaker church. He was a member of the governor's council, a member and moderator of the assembly, president of the first united colony, and deputy-governor and governor of the second When George Fox spent two months in Rhode Island in 1672, Easton was governor of the colony, but accompanied Fox almost constantly on his missionary tour His sons, Peter and John, emulated their father's civic activities, the former serving as member of the assembly and of the governor's council, attorney-general and treasurer, the latter as attorney-general for fourteen years, member of the assembly and council, deputy-governor, and governor from 1690-95 In this last position, he successfully resisted Sir William Phipps's claim to command the Rhode Island militia

Another leading Newport Quaker was Walter Clarke, who served as member of the assembly and council, twenty-three terms as deputy-governor (fifteen of them successively: from 1700-1711), and four terms as governor In this last position, he successfully withstood Governor Andros's demand for Rhode Island's precious charter, although he was at the time a member of Andros's Council for New England Not a Charter Oak, as in Hartford, but a Quaker house and Quaker diplomacy concealed and secured Rhode Island's charter. When ordered by Andros to *send* the charter, Governor Clarke declined to do so "because of the tediousness of the bad weather;" and when Andros came in person to fetch the charter, Nov. 7, 1687, Clarke sent it from his own house to his brother's, and then for Andros's benefit, caused a great search to be made for it through his own house! Following this defense of Rhode Island's fundamental constitution on parchment, Governor Clarke refused to permit the establishment or recognition of an English court of admiralty in the colony. Thus he asserted, three-quarters of a century before 1776, the American right of self-government, and based that right upon the bed-rock of charter privileges

Among other early Quaker governors were Caleb Carr, who was treasurer as well, and Henry Bull, a follower of Anne Hutchinson, a founder of Portsmouth and Newport, and builder of what was for many years Rhode Island's oldest extant house, where his wife Ann, the widow of Nicholas Easton, presided, and where many Quaker meetings were held *

Time does not suffice to tell of such early colonial Quakers of Newport as John and Joshua Coggeshall, George Lawton, Walter Newberry, Edward Thurston, Daniel and John Gould (after whom one of Narragansett's familiar islands is named); or of the later, pre-Revolutionary Quakers, whose annals are made picturesque or impressive by the beauty of Polly Lawton,** the preaching of Mary Callender, the varied

---

*This house was destroyed by fire in 1912.

**Her portrait is in the Redwood Library, and a glowing description of her beauty in the Comte de Segur's "Memoirs " Her home is now a fruit-store, on the corner of Spring and Touro Streets.

activities of the Wanton and Robinson families, the philanthropy of Abraham Redwood, and the statesmanship of Stephen Hopkins.

But a short time at least should be devoted to the coming of the English Quakers to Newport, their union with the pre-Quakers of the town, and "the things that are more excellent" for which the Newport Quakers stand in the history of the city, the state and the nation

The first Quakers to set foot on American soil were Mary Fisher and Ann Austin, who had some very trying experiences in Boston in the summer of 1656 They were despatched straight back to Barbadoes, after five weeks' imprisonment and an examination for witchcraft, and had no chance to get to Rhode Island; but the first Quaker convert in New England, Nicholas Upsall of Boston, came to Rhode Island, after he had been fined and banished for supplying ' the two Quakeresses with food while in prison, for offering to buy the one hundred "heretical books ' which they brought with them, and which the Boston hangman burned in the market-place, and for making a public protest against the first penal law which Massachusetts launched against the Quaker The eight Quakers who arrived in Boston two days after Mary Fisher and Anna Austin were expelled were also immediately placed in close confinement for eleven weeks and then sent back to England. but New England heard much of them, Samuel Gorton of Warwick invited them to settle in that town, and some of them returned as speedily as possible the next year in the Quaker Mayflower, "The Woodhouse."

This ship, so famous in Quaker annals, was regarded by its Quaker captain and passengers as a second Noah's Ark which God led, in Robert Fowler's, the courageous and pious skipper's, quaint words, "as a man leads a horse by the head;" and when, after leaving five missionaries in New Amsterdam, the remaining eleven arrived, on the 3rd of August, 1657, in Newport, they were convinced that God had led them to a second Ararat, whence they should replenish the New World, submerged by barbarism of various kinds, with a Quaker civilization. In Newport, at least, they found congenial soil among the community of Coddington and Easton, and not only did this community convert itself into the first Quaker meeting of Newport, but the town became a base of operations for both native and English Quakers in their invasion of the rest of New England.

The familiar procedure was for a company of English Friends to come to Newport, then to go with Newport Friends to Massachusetts, where they protested against the penal laws, and were imprisoned and whipped, and then to return to Rhode Island, "the habitation of the hunted-Christ," as they call it, "where we ever found a place of rest when weary we have been."

One such party, including two women, Sarah Gibbons and Dorothy Waugh, travelled on foot from Newport all the way to Salem, through the wilderness and through what appears from their description to have been a March blizzard; after a fortnight of missionary endeavor, they were whipped in Boston and sent back to Newport. Among the Salem converts on this journey, were Lawrence and Cassandra Southwick*, who fled to Shelter Island, and Joshua Buffum, who came to Rhode Island.

Another English Quakeress who made Newport a base of operations was Elizabeth Hooton, the first woman convinced by George Fox, and the first woman Friend to appear in the ministry. She suffered bitter persecution in England; sailed to Virginia and thence to Newport; gave her "testimony" in Boston, was imprisoned and then banished to Rhode Island; returned to Boston, was whipped through Cambridge, Watertown and Dedham; left in the woods during a cold night, she arrived torn and bleeding in Newport, returning to Cambridge, she was again whipped through three towns, to Rhode Island; to Boston once more, she was whipped at the cart tail through Boston, Roxbury, Dedham and Medfield, and left in the woods, travelling seventy miles on foot back to Newport, she was again refreshed, and again went to Boston!

Such were the stories that were told at Rhode Island firesides and that turned many families to join the perse-

---

*Cf Whittier's "Cassandra Southwick, 1658."

cuted *; and in such incidents the Newport Quakers were
often participators. The most familiar and most tragic of
them all was associated with Mary Dyer, Daniel Gould, and
other Friends of Newport, who went to Boston in September, 1659, with William Robinson and Marmaduke Stephenson of England, Hope Clifton, Mary and Patience Scott of
Providence (the latter an eleven years' old niece of Ann
Hutchinson) and other Rhode Island Friends, "being moved
of the Lord," as they told the Massachusetts authorities, "to
look your bloody laws in the face and to accompany those
who should suffer by them " Mary Dyer, who went repeatedly to protest against the unrighteous laws of Massachusetts,
was the wife of William Dyer, (or Dyre) of Newport, who
spent his life in upholding Rhode Island's righteous laws,
having been the first clerk of the settlement in Portsmouth,
the first secretary of united Portsmouth and Newport, the
first recorder of Providence Plantations, and attorney-general of the colony. After imprisonments and whippings, sentence of death, reprieve on the gallows, and banishment on
pain of death in case of return, Mary Dyer was at last hung
on Boston Common. Her death was doubtless more impressive to the American colonists than was that of her three
fellow martyrs, men and Englishmen as they were, and we
can well appreciate the shock which it sent through the
Quaker circles of Newport. The blood of martyrs became
the seed of the church, on this as on so many occasions; and
Edward Wanton, a citizen of Boston, who stood within the
shadow of Mary Dyer's gallows, marveling at her heroic
constancy, was converted to her faith, removed to Rhode
Island, and became the ancestor of a line of Quaker worthies, among whom were at least three governors of the Island
commonwealth. The other Rhode Islanders who accompanied Mary Dyer to Boston were imprisoned for two months

---

*Cf Whittier's "Snow-Bound "

> Then, haply, with a look more grave,
> And soberer tone, some tale she gave
> From painful Sewell's ancient tome,
> Beloved in every Quaker home,
> Of faith fire-winged by martyrdom." — — —

and then whipped, Daniel Gould receiving thirty lashes.*

John Rous, an English Quaker missionary, writing to Margaret Fell on the 3rd of September, 1658, from what he described as "the Lion's den called Boston prison," gives the following enthusiastic report "Truth is spread here above 200 miles, and many in the land are in fine conditions, and very sensible of the power of God, and walk honestly in their measures. And some of the inhabitants of the land, who are Friends, have been forth in the service and they do more grieve the enemy than we, for they have hope to be rid of us, but they have no hope to be rid of them. We keep the burden of the service off from them at present, for no sooner is there need in a place, but straightway some or other of us step to it, but, when it is the will of the Father to clear us of this land, then will the burden fall on them " After speaking of the condition of "the Seed" in Boston, Plymouth, Connecticut and New Haven, Rous reports: "We have two strong places in this land, the one at Newport in Rhode Island, and the other at Sandwich, which the enemy will never get dominion over. " The Massachusetts "enemy" tried for a score of years, especially by enforcing the notorious "Cart and Whip Act," to get dominion over the Friends, but Rous's prophecy proved true.

The first meeting-place of the Friends of Newport was the large living-room in the house of Wm. Coddington, which stood for many years on Marlborough St., opposite Duke St. The lot on which it stood was six acres in size, and bounded by Marlborough, Farewell, North Baptist and Thames Streets. In this were held the Yearly Meetings, at least until Coddington's death, and many another meeting which was too large for the house. The first Meeting House proper was built near the corner of Marlborough and Farewell Streets in 1672, and is believed to have been the first house built distinctly as a house of worship in Rhode Island.

---

*This punishment, Gould says, was inflicted upon him while he was "tyed to the carriage of a great Eam." Two other men received fifteen stripes, and the women ten stripes, each ; after which, Gould records, "we were all lead back to prison where our lodgings were with our sore backs upon the boards, where we remained until after the Execution - - - And this is my comfort to this day, and I bless God for it, that my sufferings were in great Innocence."

Its successor, on the same site, was built in 1699-1700.* The women's section was added in 1808, since which time it has retained its present form and dimensions

The following items relating to the building of the Meeting House I culled from the minutes of the Newport Monthly Meeting, Vol 1 (1676-1707-8), which are preserved in the vaults of the Newport Historical Society

P. 60 (98): At a monthly mens meeting at newport in Rhoad Island at our meeting house ye 7th Day of ye 12th moth 1698 flriends have proposed to have a meeting house Built at portsmouth and alsoe to have a Large meeting house built at new porte and ffriends are Desined to subscribe what theye are willing: ffor ye performing of of Boath (mathew Borden Gidion ffreborne John Borden and Abraham Anthony (are appynted to carey one the meeting house at portsmouth and to Receive ye colections flor that purpose and that theye doe agree wheare to Erect it and make Report to our next Monthly meeting.

Walter Clarke Ebinezer Slocum Jacob mott John Borden: are aded to Execators of Wm Edwards to maneg and take ceare of ye land bought of Ann Bull and all other consarnes Relating to the Estate of Wm Edwards wch is Left to this meeting."

P 64 (102) At a monthly mens meeting at newport at our monthly meeting house ye 27 4th mo. 1699 . This meeting hath thought convenient to choose some ffriends & appoynte ym to erect and Build a meeting house and theye consult aboufe the mater how and wheare & ye Demensions and make Returne to our next mens meeting.

John Easton: Senr Walter Clarke Edward Thurstone John Easton Junr Danl Gould John StantonTho: Cornell Lathum Clark John. Gould Wm Barker Wm Alen ffor newporte ffor cononicutt Joseph mody & Ebinezer Slocum
ffor portsmoth: Jacob mott & mathew borden

---

*This is the middle part of the present house 45 x 46 ft , with two rows of galleries, one above the other, a hipped roof, and a tower, 10 ft square and 10 ft high. It cost £261 18s 9d

and that They doe meete togeather at our meeting house ye 10th daye of ye 5th: moth: 1699. being one 2d daye of ye week.

7-19 1699 ffriends have appoynted to Laye out ye place wheare ye meeting house shal: stand & to doe it after ye meeting

8-17-1699 ffriends have Layed oute and appoynted ye place wheare ye meeting house shall stand and have brought Great Stones & other stones to Laye ye ffoundation

Quarterly Meeting at Newport, 4-4-1700. Rhoad Island monthly meeting being called one (to know what Buisiness theye have Refered to this meeting) Thomas Cornell & Jacob mot· acquainted this meeting yt some ffriends were not Sattisfied aboute ye Lanthorne, and ye new meeting house [at portsmouth]; ffriends having had much Debate in Love and condisending one to another have Left ye mater [sold Portsmouth's old meeting house to Joseph mory 3-28-1700; for 11:14; towards new house (see Minute for 5-23-1700, Books and papers of Mtg placed in care of John Easton Jr.]

8-25-1700 Thomas Cornell desires yt ffriends would appoynt some to· account with him aboute ye charge in building ye new meeting house in Newport ffriends have chosen [4]

9-12-1700 Thomas Cornell's charge presented—

	£	s	d
ye whole charge is	261.	- 18	- 9
colected by subscription	168	- 05	- 0
oute of: ffriends stock	100	- 00	- 0
	268	- 5	- 0

£ s d
The overplusse is 6· 6 3: wch is given to Thomas Cornell's wife.   .

Thomas Cornell is ordered to ffite ye old meeting house ffor this winter season

10-10-1700 Two Friends desired to "Build a shedd in ffriends yarde at new porte to sett horses under".

6-19-1701 "It is proposed to Build a meeting house at providence wch is Liked & Refered to our next mens meeting."

The records of the births, deaths and marriages of the Newport Friends begin in 1672, probably as a result of the advice of George Fox, who visited them that year. On the inside cover of the book for recording marriages is the following memorandum. "Friends two books bought at Boston cost 20 shillings, the biggest for births and Deaths, and the lesser book for marriages only. So ordered at the mans meeting of friends at the House of William Coddington in the town of New Port in Road Island in the yeare 1672, the 22th day of ye 8-m 1672." The first death recorded is that of Mary Coddington, the wife of William, in 1647, and the record is accompanied by the statement that she "was buried in the burying place of Friends that was given to the Friends by William Coddington, her husband."

The Newport Monthly Meeting was established in 1658, eighteen years before its records began; and this was soon followed by the Rhode Island Quarterly Meeting, which constituted with those of Salem and Sandwich the only three Quarterly Meetings which New England possessed before 1784. The Rhode Island Quarterly Meeting was held once in three months at Smithfield, Dartmouth, Swansea, and Greenwich, respectively, while Newport was the seat of the Yearly Meeting. This last meeting was the most important meeting in New England*, for while it was at first a large "General Meeting" for worship and fellowship only, it soon came to exercise disciplinary powers and to be the focus of all the monthly and quarterly meetings of New England. Its first session was held in Newport in 1661 at the suggestion of George Rofe, an English Friend, and was so largely attended that the Boston officials are said by a contemporary** to have "made an alarm that the Quakers were gathering to kill the people and fire the town of Boston." Until 1695, the Friends of Long Island, as well as of New England, came to Newport to attend the Yearly Meeting and we may almost say of it what Whittier said of the Quaker Alumni of the

---

*Its records date from 1683.
**Bishop's "New England Judged"

Providence School "From the well-springs of Hudson, the sea-cliffs of Maine, Grave men, sober matrons, you gather again", and we can well understand how it became for all northern Quakerism in those isolated and seemingly humdrum days the great social and educational as well as religious event of the year. The meeting's size may be estimated from the fact that by 1700 one-half of Rhode Island's population and one-third of its places of worship belonged to the Quakers. Indeed, they and the Baptists had practically preempted the colony between them, much to the disgust of the clergymen of the Church of England, one of whom complained that the Quakers turned their backs on everybody's reading of the Scriptures except their own, and were unapproachable and unyielding in matters of faith.

The Newport Yearly Meeting grew steadily until the middle of the Eighteenth century, and was especially large when some distinguished visitor was expected to be present. George Fox and six other eminent ministers attended it in 1672, and so many people flocked to it from all sides that they required two days after it was over, to take leave of all the friends they had made during its sessions*. The name of Farewell Street was again appropriate to the scene. When such men as Thomas Chalkley, John Richardson, Thomas Story, John and Samuel Fothergill, visited the meeting in later years, its attendants numbered, in 1722, 2000, and 5000 in 1743, when it was probably the largest in the world. About the end of the century, 1798, the system of definite representation in it of monthly and quarterly meetings was established, and, with a similar system in the Yearly Meetings of the South, and the pure democracy of the many monthly meetings, it rivalled the Puritan town meeting, the Cavalier county court, and the colonial assemblies, as a nursery of that government of the people, by the people, and for the people which blossomed forth nearly a century later.

---

*George Fox's "Journal", II, 160 "The glorious power of the Lord which was over all, and His blessed truth and life flowing amongst them, had so knit and united them together that they spent two days in taking leave of one another and of the Friends of the Island, and then, being mightily filled with the presence and power of the Lord, they went away with joyful hearts to their various habitations "

Roger Williams attended the Newport Yearly Meeting in 1671, and was moved to make some comment on the doctrine he had heard; but he was "stopt", he says, "by the sudden praying of the Governor's wife [Ann, the wife of Nicholas Easton]". He stood up again, and again he was "stopt by John Burnett's [Burnyeat's] sudden falling to prayer and dismissing the assembly".* He did not come to the meeting the next year when George Fox and his companions were there; but they went to Providence and held two large meetings, one of them in "a greate barne", says Fox, "which was soe full of people, yt I was extremely soaked with sweat, but all was well". All was wrong, Roger Williams thought, and he challenged Fox to debate fourteen propositions, or accusations against the Quakers, with him. This challenge was not received by Fox until he had left Newport on his way south, but it was accepted by some of his associates whom Williams calls "His Holiness, George Fox's Journeymen and Chaplains"

The debate was arranged in a visit which the Friends made to Williams's home in Providence, and the day before it was to be held in Newport the sturdy septuagenarian rowed thirty miles down the Bay to engage in it. "God graciously helped me", he says, "in rowing all day with my old bones so that I got to Newport toward the midnight before the morning appointed." He had engaged to debate his propositions with all comers, and encountered three Quaker champions, and, before great crowds of listeners, with Governor Easton presiding and maintaining "the civil peace", the theological, ecclesiastical and at times personal debate waxed and waned throughout three long summer days. It must have been a strange scene to any eyes, and doubly so to ours accustomed in Newport to contests of such different kinds,—tennis, yachting, polo, dog-shows, etc,—which was enacted down on Marlborough Street in those quaint old colonial times. Providence was jealous of Newport's good fortune, and it was accordingly arranged that half of the debate should be held in that town. The audience, or a large part of it, appears to have accompanied the

* "George Fox Digged out of his Burrowes"

debaters to Providence, but a single day was sufficient then to end it Leave to print was given to the respective contestants, and Roger Williams issued his "George Fox Digged out of his Burrowes", while the Friends replied in "A New England Firebrand Quenched".* John Burnyeat says in his "Journal"**. "It would be tedious here to insert the Discourse [that is, an account of the debate in Newport], if I were able; but I cannot remember it. There is a Book in Manuscript, of what was taken in Short-hand of the Discourse at that present."

It is probably fortunate that the Ms. Book is not well known; for judging from expressions in the printed books, the debate was probably at times bitter and undignified Roger Williams, for example, characterizes William Edmondson, one of the Quaker champions, as having "A flash of wit, a face of Brass, and a Tongue set on fire from the Hell of Lyes and Fury"; while Edmondson calls Williams "an old Priest and an enemy of Truth, - - - a bitter old man - - - full of Weakness, Folly and Envy against the Truth and the Friends."

More pleasing is it for us to recall the meeting at Newport in more kindly years between Channing and Whittier and the English Friend, Joseph Sturge, when—

"No bars of sect or clime were felt,—
  The Babel strife of tongues had ceased,—
And at one common altar knelt
  The Quaker and the Priest." ***

Theological controversy, however, was like the breath of life in the Seventeenth and Eighteenth Centuries, and the Newport Friends showed their recognition of its importance by engaging James Franklin, Benjamin's brother, who became the first printer in Newport in 1729, to issue as one of his first books Robert Barclay's "Apology for the True

---

*Staples believes that this was written chiefly by Richard Scott, ' the first Friend in Providence."

**P. 53

***Whittier's "Channing."

Christian Divinity, as the same is set forth and preached by
the people called in scorn Quakers ' *

But the Quakers of the olden times,—as they "walked
with noiseless feet the round of uneventful years, and o'er
and o'er they sowed the spring and reaped the autumn
ears",—realized in every successive day's experience that

"From scheme and creed the light goes out,
    The saintly fact survives :
The blessed Master none can doubt
    Revealed in Holy lives "

And we believe that the early Friends of Newport strove,
in spite of human weakness and defects, so to live that when
they left this island home they should leave it in some slight
measure "hallowed by pure lives and tranquil deaths " Like
their fellows elsewhere, they were Puritans of an advanced
type, and set up in their "advices," "queries," "family visits,"
and meetings for discipline and worship, a standard of morality which gave first place to honesty, sobriety and simplicity. This led them to insist on the strict keeping of promises
in business, and to punish such business practices as "the
salting up unmerchantable beef and exposing it for sale;"
also to denounce lotteries, at a time when even churches and
colleges depended upon this, now admittedly, dishonest
source of revenue; to deprecate "fiddling, dancing and card-
playing," at a time when these were almost the sole and the
universal diversion of youth and age alike, but when they so
often led to evil habits, and to moderate the strong, natural
desire to "follow the fashion " Wigs,—or "Perry Wiggs," as
they spelled and called them,—gave them an inordinate
amount of trouble One meeting, for example, expressed its
sentiments on this, at that time, capital article of apparel as
follows "All Friends who suppose that they have need of
wiggs ought to take the advice and approbation of the vis-
itors [that is, the overseers] of their respective [monthly]
meetings before they proceed to get one And it is the tender
advice and brotherly request of this Meeting that all be care-

*This is the 6th Edition in English , a copy of it is in the Redwood
Library, and a copy is in the Historical Society   Franklin also printed, in
Newport in 1752, Barclay's "Catechism "

ful to observe the same, and not in a careless or overly-
minded cutt of their hair (which is given them for a covering) to put on a wigg or indecent capp which has been observed of late years to be a growing practice among too
many of the young men in several parts, to the trouble of
many honest Friends, it plainly appearing (in some) for a
imitation and joyning with the spirit and fashion of the
world."

As early as 1673, the monthly, quarterly, and yearly
meetings of Rhode Island began to oppose the use, manufacture, sale or gift of alcoholic liquors, except for medicinal
purposes, and thus gave an early impulse to the prohibition
wave which is running high in our time, both in peace and
in war It was not only for their own members that they
were thus concerned. The Yearly Meeting of 1784, for example, passed the following minute "We entreat that they
[the members of the Society in New England] forbear the
said practices that a line may in due time be drawn, and the
standard be raised and spread to the nation."

The Quaker testimony against the taking of oaths,
whether as an expletive in private conversation or in judicial
procedure, received recognition in Rhode Island from the
very beginning, and affirmation was permitted in their stead
In this too, the nation has followed the Quaker lead, to which
Rhode Island's Quaker Government gave such early prestige.

The great curse of the slave-trade, domestic and foreign,
and of slave ownership, was a truly formidable one for the
Quakers to grapple with, especially perhaps in Newport,
which was of such commercial importance, and in Rhode
Island, where slavery existed on a relatively large scale

From the beginnings of the Society, the meetings dealt
severely with their members for any case of cruel treatment
of their slaves, and insisted on a treatment of them consistent
with humanity and religion

Rhode Island's Quaker governor, Walter Clarke, refused
to permit his colony to participate in New England's sale of
Indian prisoners into slavery, after King Philip's War, in
1676, and procured the passage of a law providing that "no
Indian in this colony be a slave."

As early as 1717, the Yearly Meeting in Newport began

to oppose both the trade in and ownership of negro slaves
After the painful efforts of two generations of such Quaker
opponents of slavery as "College Tom" Hazard of South
Kingstown, and the saintly John Woolman, of New Jersey,
and as a result of the even more painful "dealings" of the various New England monthly meetings with their slave-owning
members (such as Stephen Hopkins, for example, and
Joshua Rathbun), the Newport Yearly Meeting in 1773 was
able at last to wipe the stain of the iniquitous system entirely from its skirts The next year, 1774, the Yearly Meeting
appointed a committee to work for abolition in Rhode
Island, and had the satisfaction in the same year of seeing
one of its former members, Stephen Hopkins, draft Rhode
Island's act against the further enslavement of negroes within its borders The Yearly Meeting's gratification at this event
was probably increased by the reflection that its distinguished member, who was nine times governor of the colony,
had been "disowned" by Smithfield Monthly Meeting because he would not yield to Friends in the freeing of his one
slave woman

Thus the Newport and Rhode Island Friends bore an
honorable part in that colonial movement for abolition
which was to become, through a long course of moral, political and industrial education, a great national reality.

The Quaker "testimony" which appears to be of most
public interest in the present day is the rejection of war
as a means of settling disputes between and among nations
and the substitution for it of a more civilized and effective
means. Newport Quaker history sheds much instructive light
upon this great world-problem, and a bare glimpse of it
must be given here in concluding this over-long address.

The use of "carnal" weapons the Quakers have rejected
from the beginning of their history, both as wrong in itself
and as fatal to the success of those "spiritual" weapons
which alone they regard as right and effective. In their efforts to keep their members up to this standard, the meetings have "labored with" or "disowned" many a "fighting
Quaker," like the favorite general of Washington in the Revolution. Nathaniel Greene of Warwick, Rhode Island, and
Jacob Browne of Bucks County, Pennsylvania, who held high

command in the War of 1812. In spite of such distinguished delinquents, the Society as a whole has kept its ancient testimony bright and untarnished, and accepts with due appreciation our national government's recognition of it during the present great war. It is a cause of gratification to many Friends today that the Society has strenuously endeavored to persuade the government to place this exemption, not upon corporate membership, but solely upon individual conscience, and that it has in some small measure succeeded in its endeavor. While the Quakers in the colonies suffered much by fine and imprisonment for refusing to "train" and to bear arms in Queen Anne's, King George's, and the French and Indian wars, Rhode Island set a better example under its Quaker governor, Nicholas Easton, by passing, on the 13th of August, 1673, an act exempting from military service those who were opposed to it for conscience' sake. "The inhabitants of this colony," declares this deservedly famous act, "have a conscience against exacting an oath, ... how much more ought such men forbear to compel their equal neighbors against their conscience to trayne to fight and to kill . . . Bee it therefore enacted by his Majesty's authority, that noe person (within this Colony), that is or hereafter shall be persuaded in his conscience that he cannot or ought not to trayne, to learne to fight, nor to war, nor kill any person or persons, shall at any time be compelled against his judgment and conscience to trayne, arm, or fight, to kill any person or persons by reason of or at the command of any officer of this Collony, civil or military, nor by reason of any by-law here past or formerly enacted; nor shall any suffer any punishment, fine, distraint, penalty, nor imprisonment, who cannot in conscience traine, fight, nor kill any person nor persons for the aforesaid reasons "

This sweeping exemption for conscience' sake was passed just before King Philip's War, and when that war became imminent the Quakers of Newport endeavored their utmost to prevent it and to settle the respective grievances of the Indians and the English by means of arbitration. William Coddington was governor at the time, and doubtless at his suggestion a committee of five members of the Rhode Island assembly, with John Easton, Junior, the

Quaker deputy-governor at their head, rowed up to King Philip's headquarters at Mount Hope and argued and plead an entire day with him and his chieftains in behalf of arbitration "We told them," Easton records in his "Narrative," "that our desire was that the quarrel might be rightly decided in the best way, not as dogs decide their quarrels." The Indians frankly "owned that fighting was the worst way, but they inquired how right might take place without fighting We said by arbitration. They said that by arbitration the English agreed against them, and so by arbitration they had much wrong . . . We said they might chuse a Indian King and the English might chuse the Governor of New Yorke, that neither had case [should have cause] to say that either wear parties to the difference. They said they had not heard of this way "

The Quaker pleader doubtless also reminded the Indians of the mutual justice and friendship which had existed for so long in Rhode Island between them and the English, and of the fact that his father, Governor Nicholas Easton, had recently provided that one-half of the jury in trials where Indians were involved should be Indians, and that the evidence of Indians should be accepted as equal with that of an Englishman. But the Indians remembered the Pequot War and many another sad and sorry incident in the relations between the Indians and the English outside of Rhode Island, and feared to entrust their case to arbitration. "We were persuaded," Easton concludes, "that if this way had been tendered [by the other colonies] they would have accepted "*

A half-dozen years later, another Quaker inaugurated in Pennsylvania his Holy Experiment, which included among other illustrious American principles and practices the great method of arbitration and judicial settlement in place of war It is of much interest to the student of Rhode Island's history to find thus early the statesmanlike policy which, adopted by Penn in Pennsylvania in 1682, and ad-

---

*For a more detailed account of this episode, Cf. an article in the *Friends Intelligencer*, for Eleventh Month 3, 1917, entitled "The Peace Programme of Rhode Island Friends, 1675," by Wm I Hull

vocated by him in his great "Essay" of 1693 for application to the war-worn Europe of his time, became the corner-stone of our American republic, and under the auspices of the Hague Conference is destined to become the accepted and habitual practice of the nations.

In view of these and other still waters of life which flowed through the Quaker centers of colonial Newport and Rhode Island, some small part of which has been but faintly reflected in this address, I trust that it is not too much to claim with the modest Whittier:

"No honors of war to our worthies belong,
  Their plain stem of life never flowered into song :
  But the fountains they opened still gush by the way,
  And the world for their healing is better to-day"

Rev. Dr. SAMUEL HOPKINS

A Paper read before the Newport Historical Society
February 6th, 1917

By

Rev. CLARIS EDWIN SILCOX

SAMUEL HOPKINS

In one of his earliest and most fascinating books, Friedrich Nietzsche, the *enfant terrible* of German philosophy, wrote: "Every man and nation needs a certain knowledge of the past, whether it be through monumental, antiquarian, or critical history, according to his objects, powers and necessities." "History is necessary . . to the man of action and power who fights a great fight and needs examples, teachers and comforters . . . . It . . . shows us how to bear steadfastly the reverses of fortune, by reminding us of what others have suffered " This is its monumental function. Next, Nietzsche says, "history is necessary to the man of conservative and reverent nature who looks back to the origins of his existence with love and trust; through it, he gives thanks for life The possession of his ancestor's furniture changes its meaning in his soul, for his soul is rather possessed by it. All that is small and limited, mouldy and obsolete, gains a worth and inviolability of its own from the   soul of the antiquary migrating into it, and building a secret nest there. The history of the town becomes the history of himself; he looks on the walls, the turreted gates, the town council, the fair, as an illustrated diary of his youth, and sees himself in it all . . He greets the soul of his people from afar as his own, across the dim and troubled centuries; his gifts and his virtues he in such power of feeling and divination, his scent of a half-vanished trail, his instinctive correctness in reading the scribbled past." Such is the antiquarian use of history. And finally, says Nietzsche, is the scholar's, or critical, use of history. Here the past is brought to the bar of judgment, is interrogated remorselessly, and finally condemned. "Every past," said the philosopher, "is worth condemning."

Now, our attitude tonight in considering the life and work of Samuel Hopkins, is three-fold in its nature. We shall approach him with the love of the antiquary, because Hopkins was an important figure in the history of this town at its most interesting period, viz., from 1770 to the first years of the nineteenth century. We shall also look to him for inspiration, for he is an inspiring figure, heroic, harmonizing in himself the moral severity of the Puritan with a Christ-like passion for the souls and well-being of men. And we shall try to be critical, not only of the man, but also of the age, praising what is worthy of praise and modestly censuring that which deserves criticism.

For the benefit of such as may not be conversant with the outstanding facts in the life of Hopkins, it may be said that he was not a native of Newport, but came here in 1770 and until the day of his death in December, 1803, was minister of the First Congregational Church in this city Thus for thirty-three years he was associated with the history of this town, preaching in the old church now used as an auction room on Mill street, and living in the house almost directly opposite the Union Congregational Church on Division street. After the Revolutionary war, when his own church was too badly damaged to be used for Divine worship, and until sufficient funds had been collected to repair it, his congregation met in this meeting-house* which was large enough for his diminished and impoverished people. In Newport he wrote his System of Divinity which was published in 1792 and created a great stir not only 'in Newport but even in England and Scotland and won for its many distinguishing views the name "Hopkinsian" or "Hopkintonian." These views were in reality a modification of the Calvinistic position and were considered heretical and worthy of classification under St. Paul's "philosophy and vain deceit" by a large number of ministers and theologians. Hopkins died and was buried here; and when the First and Second Congregational Churches united and built their place of worship on the present site of the United Congregational Church, his bones were reverently disinterred and re-buried

---

*The Seventh Day Baptist, in which this address was delivered

to the south of the church, where those interested may still see and decipher the following inscription:

IN MEMORY OF
SAMUEL HOPKINS, D D
Pastor of the
First Congregational Church
in Newport,
Who departed this life
Dec. 20th, A. D. 1803,
In the 83rd year of his age;
Whose faithful attention to the duties
of his pastoral office, and
whose valuable writings,
will recommend his character
when this monument,
erected by his bereaved flock,
shall, with the precious dust it covers,
cease to be distinguished.

For the benefit of those who may desire to pursue their studies of Hopkins further, it is perhaps well to mention the following books:

Autobiography.
Memoir of the Life and Character of the Rev'd Samuel Hopkins, D D —John Ferguson, (1830)
Life of Samuel Hopkins, by William Patten
Memoir of the Life and Character of Hopkins, by Edwards A Park (1854).
Essay on Hopkins in "Old Portraits" by John Greenleaf Whittier (1847).
The Works of Samuel Hopkins, edited by Park, 1854 (Three volumes)

There are many other references to his theology, but these are the books of greatest general interest.

Samuel Hopkins, the object of this sketch, was the son of Timothy Hopkins and Mary Judd, of Waterbury, Conn., where he was born, the eldest of a family of 5 sons and 4 daughters, on September 17, 1721. He was born on the Sabbath Day and baptized soon after his birth. When his father was assured that his son would live, he promised that he should be given a college training and fitted to be a sabbath-day man, or minister. We know little of his youth, beyond what he tells us in his Autobiography. He did not recall ever hearing a profane word until he had reached the fifteenth year of his age, which is a sure testimony to the Christian environment in which his early years were spent. Hopkins says

> "I from my youth was not volatile and wild, but rather of a sober and steady make, and was not guilty of external irregularities, such as disobedience to parents, profanation of the sabbath, lying, foolish jesting, quarrelling, passion and anger, or rash and profane words, and was disposed to be diligent and faithful in whatever business I was employed"

He admits, however, that he was generally careless "about invisible things . and sometimes, though rarely, had some serious thoughts of God" Once he had a dream in which he and his brother two years his junior were driven down to hell with the rest of the wicked, and sentenced to everlasting misery. "This greatly impressed my mind," says Hopkins, "for a long time after"

It is unfortunate that Hopkins in his autobiography did not tell us more about his youth, but he was interested in little beyond his religious experience. It seems inconceivable that a theologian must always be a theologian from his cradle, and it would be reassuring to know that Hopkins occasionally played games with his brothers and sisters and shook with laughter, perchance, upon the occasion of their discomfort But he lived in days which are hard to reconstruct, in which the children of pious households were early made to realize the terror of the Lord, and where the only happiness recorded seems to have been that of contemplating the goodness of God and the beauties of heaven.

In his Life of President Jonathan Edwards, Hopkins tells a story which is certainly characteristic of the time.

When Jonathan Edwards was a boy, he with some other lads, built a hut in the swamp where they were wont to gather together. Surely this savours of perennial boyhood. Some of the gentlemen here may, in their youth, have had some favorite resort, a hut or a cave, to which they resorted with their playmates. But it is very doubtful if the purpose of their juvenile assembly was identical with that of the companions of Jonathan Edwards. He and his 'pals' went out to this swamp-hut to pray. When we are estimating the influences that made the religious revival of the early half of the eighteenth century possible, let us not forget this hut in the swamp and its purpose. Samuel Hopkins may not have had experiences identical with his friend, Jonathan, but he was brought up in a very pious home where he had ample reason to reflect upon the possibilities of his own salvation.

In 1737, when he was sixteen years of age, he was admitted to Yale College, then under the presidency of Elisha Williams. The dominant studies, non-elective, were logic, physics, mathematics, ethics, rhetoric and theology. Such studies were inclined to develop originality of thought rather than felicity of expression,* and the intellectual discipline to which Yale submitted Hopkins must have contributed largely to his fondness for abstract thinking, but we must not forget that theologians are born, and not made. They are probably pre-destined before the foundation of the world.

Hopkins tells us that while a member of the college he "had the character of a sober, studious youth, and of a better scholar than the bigger half of the members of that society; and had the approbation of the governors of the college." He adds: "I avoided the intimacy and the company of the openly vicious; and indeed kept but little company, being

---

*President Woolsey of Yale said in an address delivered August 14, 1850: "The effect of the modern system of education, or of society, or of both, is to repress originality of thinking, to destroy individual peculiarities, and to produce in general sameness among those whom it educates." (Quoted by Professor Park in the Memoir of Hopkins). Thus we perceive that the fallacy of the current educational theory endureth from generation to generation. It could not be said of the curriculum to which Hopkins was submitted that it repressed originality of thinking.

attentive to my studies " He desired to be known as a pious
youth, and sometime before 1740 he joined the church at
Waterbury, although he afterwards feared that he had no
positive experience of saving grace at the time. Of course,
we must remember that conversion was at that time considered to be something catastrophic and revolutionary, as it is
still considered by some, although modern thought lays
more emphasis upon the culture of religion than upon conviction of sin. In 1740 George Whitefield visited Yale and
preached to the people of New Haven He made a great impression, people travelling twenty miles to hear him. Most
of his hearers approved of him. Hopkins, too, heard and
approved, although like so many hearers, he seemed to apply
the judgments of the great evangelist to others rather than
to himself. "He preached against mixed dancing and frolic-
ing of males and females together; which practice was then
very common in New England This offended some, especially young people But I remember I justified him in this
in my own mind, and in conversation with those who were
disposed to condemn him "

Early in the next year, Gilbert Tennant came to New
Haven from Boston, and preached there with a "remarkable
and mighty power Thousands were awakened, and many
cried out with distress and horror of mind, under a conviction of God's anger, and their constant exposedness to
endless destruction." The students who were professing
Christians before they came to college, such as young David
Brainerd, busied themselves in personal work among the
other students, canvassing them in their rooms and asking
them to accept Christ and His salvation. Brainerd came to
visit Hopkins, although Hopkins was a senior and Brainerd
only a sophomore; but Hopkins purposely refused to com-
mit himself Nevertheless, he was not untouched In such
a great revival of religious interest, men naturally take sides
It is a case of being "for" or "against", just as we have
observed in the recent Billy Sunday phenomenon in New
England. The thoughts of Hopkins at this time were long,
long thoughts.

But if Hopkins had been impressed with Mr. Tennant
and considered his sermons to be "apples of gold in pictures

of silver," he was more impressed with the preaching of Jonathan Edwards who came to Yale in September of 1741 and spoke on "The Trial of Spirits." He concluded that if he were to study for the ministry he would do so with Mr. Edwards The character of this great preacher and his style is, perhaps, too well known to deserve quotation; nevertheless, as it has been said that he is the only American worthy of comparison with Danté*, two paragraphs are not amiss, one from his private journal describes his happiness in the contemplation of God.

"After this, my sense of divine things gradually increased, and became more and more lively, and had more than inward sweetness The appearance of everything was altered, there seem'd to be as it were a calm, sweet Cast, or appearance of divine Glory, in almost everything God's excellency, His wisdom, his purity and love, seemed to appear in everything; in the sun, moon, and stars, in the clouds and blue sky, in the grass, flowers and trees, in the water and in all nature; which used greatly to fix my mind. I often used to sit and view the moon for a long time, and so in the daytime spent much time in viewing the clouds and sky, to behold the sweet glory of God in these things, in the meantime, singing forth with a low voice my contemplations of the Creator and Redeemer, And scarce anything, among all the works of nature, was so sweet to me as thunder and lightning; Formerly nothing had been so terrible to me I used to be a person uncommonly terrified with thunder, and it used to strike me with terror, when I saw a thunder storm rising But now, on the contrary, it rejoyced me I felt God at the first appearance of a thunder-storm And used to take the opportunity at such times, to fix myself and view the clouds, and see the lightnings play, and hear the

*A statement recently made in Newport by Prof Bliss Perry

majestick and awful voice of God's thunder,
which oftentimes was exceeding entertaining,
leading me to sweet contemplation of my great
and glorious God.   And while I viewed, used to
spend my time, as it always seem'd natural to
me, to sing or chant forth my meditations, to
speak my thoughts in soliloquies and speak
with a singing voice."

The other quotation reveals the preacher's power in describing the terrors of eternal punishment   It is the concluding paragraph of the famous sermon on "Sinners in the
Hand of an Angry God," and when this was preached in
Enfield, it is said that some of the hearers were so frightened
that they jumped out of the window.   Need one wonder?
Listen.

"The God that holds you over the pit of hell
—much as one holds a spider or some loath-
some insect over the fire—abhors you, and is
dreadfully provoked.   His wrath towards you
burns like fire,   He looks upon you as being
worthy of nothing else but to be cast into the
fire.   He is of purer eyes than to bear to have
you in his sight;   you are ten thousand times
more abominable in his eyes than the most
hateful venomous serpent is in ours   You have
offended Him infinitely more than ever a stub-
born rebel did his prince;   and yet it is nothing
but his hand that holds you from falling into
the fire every moment.   It is to be ascribed to
nothing else that you did not go to hell the last
night;   that you was suffered to wake again in
this world, after you closed your eyes to sleep
And there is no other reason to be given why
you have not dropped into hell since you arose
in the morning, but that God's hand has held
you up.   There is no other reason to be given
why you have not gone to hell since you have
sat here in the house of God, provoking his pure
eyes by your sinful wicked manner of attending

his solemn worship. Yea, there is nothing else
to be given as a reason why you do not at this
very moment drop into hell."

Here, surely, is powerful preaching Here is the personal application; here the divine urgency. And when
Hopkins had received his diploma from Yale and had spent
a short time at home resting, he went to Northampton and
for four months studied theology and the duties of the
pastoral office with this mighty New England divine. Later,
Hopkins edited the works of Edwards and wrote a memoir
of him He was licensed to preach on April 29, 1742

He then received invitations to preach as a candidate for many "comfortable" pulpits, but the first that he
considered seriously was the parish at Great Barrington, or,
as it was known in the days of Hopkins, Housatonick
Housatonick was then on the verge of the wilderness, and
consisted of more sinners than saints. It was a heterogeneous community, partly Puritan, partly Dutch, on the very
frontiers of the New England settlement, encircled by Indians not always friendly and settled by pioneers of the daredevil type. It was probably the last place under God's
heaven for a man like Samuel Hopkins, fundamentally a
student and a thinker, to go. He himself hesitated a long
time. In his journal he wrote. "The circumstances of this
place appear more and more dreadful to me There seems
to be no religion here. If I did not think I had a call here, I
should be quite discouraged."

'Though he received an invitation to found a church
there and be its pastor and teacher, he was offered only 60
pounds for settlement, and 35 pounds a year with the increase of 20 shillings a year until the maximum of 45 pounds
a year had been reached. He did not see how he could live
on it and he told them so, but he felt that this community
needed the Gospel. It seemed that it was his duty to accept
the call and so he expressed his willingness to remain there
on November 25, 1743 He was ordained on the 28th of the
following month, and there he remained and labored, "on
the edge of cultivation" until January 18, 1769, or for 25
years and 21 days.

He had his own troubles,for there were few tangible
evidences of the results of his ministry. He did succeed in
getting five men to be the charter members of the church,
but he saw no signs of any genuine conversion for seven
years when a certain H.D. showed symptoms of real religion,
and straightway died. But we must remember that our theologian was very slow to acknowledge the genuineness of
any professed conversion as the following episode will
testify. The minister had been summoned to the bedside of
a dying woman who was "full of joy and comfort," supposing she had saving discoveries of Christ. "She admired
the goodness of God, and called upon all to praise Him. Upon
examining her, I was satisfied she was deceived, that it was
only the workings of her imagination. She was confident,
but I told her my fears! How exposed to the delusions of
the devil are ignorant persons!"

In the light of this passage, we may fairly assume that
Hopkins would have had more converts had he lowered his
standards. But his rigor, and sincerity—in his later years
he was nicknamed "Old Sincerity"—made him relentless,
an opponent of the "Half-way Covenant," so common at the
time, he refused to baptize the children of all but the regen-
erate; consequently, a number of the "unregenerate"
clubbed together and invited an Episcopal clergyman to
come to Great Barrington and baptize their infants, which
he did. Henceforth, Hopkins found himself confronted not
only by his theological opponents outside of Housatonick,
for his views on the half-way covenant had aroused much
resentment, but also by many in his own parish, especially
the Dutchmen whom he could not understand, the Tories
whom he knew too well, and the Episcopalians whom he
loathed. He fought a good fight, but it was too much for
him. Many of his parishioners turned Churchmen, apparently, as Hopkins said, "to get rid of paying anything for the
support of the gospel." In spite of their efforts, his church
could not raise his salary. The Tories got control of the
town meeting, and threatened to withhold part of his
salary, if not all. "If they prevail," said Hopkins, "it seems
I am done here. 'The Lord reigns! Let the earth rejoice.'"

Hopkins hesitated between staying on and preaching

the true and "lively" word gratuitously, earning his living by farming; and leaving them for some other parish, where he could secure the leisure required for his studies. Eventually, he felt forced to resign, and on January 18, 1769, the pastoral relationship was terminated.

Four years after his settlement in Great Barrington, he had married a wife, a Miss Joanna Ingersol, a member of his parish who, in spite of consumptive tendencies, was spared to live with him until her death in August, 1793 He had been twice engaged before, but both engagements had been broken by the ladies in question, one of them upon the occasion of the return to town of a former suitor, when she informed him that "however much she respected him, she could not fulfill her engagement to him from the heart." Let us hope that even this affliction was overruled both for the good of the lady and of Dr. Hopkins. Dr Hopkins had eight children, three daughters and five sons. Upon the death of his wife in 1793, he married a Newport woman* who survived him.

During his twenty-five years in Housatonick he had not only admitted to his church 116 members, 71 from the world and 45 from other churches, but he had also done extensive preaching among the Indians, through an interpreter, and one of his sermons to them which has been preserved was as simple and free from metaphysics as most of his published discourses are abstract His experience with the Indians made him realize the tragedy of the juxtaposition of a superior and inferior race, and probably influenced him when he proposed the transportation of blacks to Africa and the establishment of colonies for them on the Guinea coast But to that we must refer later

Mr Hopkins was now without a church; he was suggested for Old South in Boston, also for Topham, Me, and finally, for the First Church in Newport, then vacant. He came to Newport to preach in July of 1769, and was heard for five Sabbaths. At a meeting of the church held in August, a call was extended to him, seven voting in favor of his coming, three against, and two refrained. Straightway

*Miss Elizabeth West.

his theological enemies stirred up trouble against him A pamphlet against him was circulated very widely. Letters were sent to Dr Ezra Stiles, then minister of the Second Church, evidently inviting his intervention to prevent the First Church from consummating the call. Two of these letters deserve quotation: the first is from Dr. Chauncy Whittelsey of New Haven

> "New Haven, September 17, 1769
> Reverend and Dear Sir
> Mr Hopkins, I think, expects to settle among you I esteem him a man of good sense, but I don't at all like the cast of his divinity. I have read most of his published writings, and heretofore heard him converse somewhat. His divinity does not seem to be adapted to the capacities of the vulgar, nor does it appear to me to give the most honorable character of that Being to whom all honor is due. His notions of baptism, if he insisted upon them, would increase the Church of England, or your congregation, perhaps both."

The other letter is from Charles Chauncy, dated Boston, November 14, 1769.

> "I am sorry with my whole soul that Mr Hopkins is like to settle in Newport I have a much worse opinion of his principles than of Sandeman's. He is a troublesome, conceited, obstinate man He preached away almost his whole congregation at Barrington, and was the occasion of setting up the Church of England there He will preach away all his congregation at Newport, or make them tenfold worse than they are at present. I wish his instalment could be prevented. I can add no more but that I am your good friend and brother,
> CHARLES CHAUNCY."*

*Letters quoted in the Literary Diary of Dr Stiles

Whether or not Dr Stiles surreptitiously endeavored to prevent his coming to Newport, the fact remains that on March 12, 1770, the church reconsidered its call; thirty-three voted for a call to him, and 36 against. When Mr. Hopkins was apprised of their decision, he took it with Christian forti- tude and charity, and stated that if they were unable to secure a supply for the following Sunday, he would be glad to preach for them before leaving the city permanently. As no supply had been obtained, his offer was accepted; in the course of his sermon he greatly moved his people by his defence of his theological opinions, many were seen to weep, and the church again changed its mind and asked him to be their minister. He accepted and was duly installed, Dr Ezra Stiles preaching the ordination sermon on "Saving Knowledge,"* in which the learned divine quoted Greek and Hebrew and Latin with ease, probably with considerable edification to himself, if to no one else

The second church instructed their representatives at the installing council to ask Mr. Hopkins this question "Whether he considered it a sin for the unregenerate to use the means of grace." When Mr Hopkins said that he believed the unregenerate ought to go to church and read the Bible and engage in prayer, they were quite contented and did not stand longer in the way of his installation But apparently his attitude on the matter of infant baptism had been interpreted by many as equivalent to a denial of the right of all but the elect to the means of grace.

The change from the yeomanry of the Berkshires to the seafaring folk of Rhode Island was great, for Newport was at this time not only a centre of wealth and commerce, but also of culture The census of 1774 gave the population of the town at 9,209, but this is considered an underestimation. The population has been estimated at 11,000. The popula- tion of Boston at this time was probably about 16,000,† and that of New York somewhat over 21,000. Thus it will be seen that Newport ranked with the first towns on the conti-

---

*This sermon was afterward published, and remains a dreadful warning to those who persist in carrying their lexicons into the pulpit.

†In a Mss in the possession of the United Congregational Church, Dr. Stiles gives the population of Boston in 1752 as 15,684.

nent It was noted not only for its scenery, "but also for the beauty of its private residences, for its fashionable and luxurious, as well as its intelligent and enterprising society, its culture of the fine arts, its scientific clubs, its refinement of taste and manners" There was much variety of religious opinion, Dr. McSparran having said in 1752 that "neither Epiphanius's nor Sir Richard Blackmore's catalogues contain more heterodox and different opinions in religion than are to be found in this little corner" And Professor Park, commenting on the settlement of Dr Hopkins, asks· "He could not harmonize with the Dutch farmers, what will he do with the French fashions? He was too severe for the moderate Calvinists of Connecticut and Massachusetts, will he not be a foreign element among the formalists and dilettanti of Newport?"

Nevertheless, he did manage to get along very well. The church grew He gave it a new impulse in many directions, including new rules of ecclesiastical order and a new creed, new arrangements for the care of the poor and the ordering of the church music. His Thursday night lectures were well attended He would speak to the young men one week and to the young women the next The average attendance of the young men was 40; that of the young women was 70, and this endeavor to apprise the junior members of his parish of the fundamentals of the Christian faith was successful, as there were many applicants for church membership It is not impossible that there was wisdom in his dividing the sexes; those who came to these lectures did so from a sense of religious duty rather than of social opportunity

He soon was able to establish friendly relations with Dr. Stiles of the Second Church of whom Dr Channing said "This country has perhaps not produced a more learned man." In his diary, Dr. Stiles wrote: "As the providence of God has brought us into a connection, I determined to learn and gather all the good I could from him, treat him with respect and benevolence, and endeavor as far as we agreed to co-operate with him in building up the Redeemer's kingdom, and we lived together in peace and love" Indeed, when Dr. Hopkins was absent, Dr. Stiles occasionally held union

services and preached to both congregations. He was, further, a regular attendant at the mid-week lectures On one
occasion, Dr Hopkins suffered from a severe nosebleed in
the course of his address, and as it could not be stopped, he
asked Dr. Stiles to continue the lecture. And it is recorded
that "furnished to all good works, he took the same text and
preached extemporaneously."

But the day of trouble was at hand Both Dr Stiles and
Dr Hopkins were Whigs and in 1776 it became advisable to
leave Newport Dr Stiles left in March and later became
President of Yale. Dr. Hopkins remained until December,
the month the British troops arrived in Newport, and only
then did he depart. During the next four years, he preached
in Newburyport, Mass, Stamford Conn, and other places
as opportunity offered, and returned to Newport in the
spring of 1780 He found his parsonage destroyed, his
church in a frightful condition, having been used as a barracks and hospital Pulpit and pews were gone, together
with its bell, which the British had taken away with them
when they evacuated the town The windows were smashed
or lost, and the money was not available to make the necessary repairs. Only Trinity Church escaped the ruthless
behavior of the soldiery Dr. Hopkins further found all
his wealthy families scattered or impoverished, and the situation was dark for a man sixty years of age But he did not
waver He first gathered the remnant of his parishioners
around him in a private house, and then the Seventh-Day
Baptist Meeting-House was used for his services For a time
members of the Second Church attended his services, but as
soon as they could they secured a pastor of their own

Dr. Hopkins wrote to Boston and Newburyport, seeking
funds to rehabilitate his church, and to some extent he was
successful But receiving no salary, he was forced to live
simply on what found its way to the collection plate, and the
frightful prices of the day compelled him, much against his
will, to use some of the money he had collected for repairing
the church to meet his own needs, the church justifying him
in his course It was a trying time for him, but his brave,
courageous spirit kept him up and he stood by his duty even
at great personal sacrifice and suffering. The next years

saw the writing and publication (in 1794) of his "System of Divinity," which is his one monumental work and for which he received the sum of $900. He straightway gave $100 to a missionary society which he had lately organized

But the people were poor and, like Martha, anxious over many things; and the sojourn of the French troops had leavened Newport society with the scepticism of the days of the great encyclopaedists. Dr Hopkins might give himself to his theology and to great social reforms, but his church existed at only a poor dying rate

It has been said that Hopkins's preaching diminished the congregation   But the fundamental factor in this unfortunate diminution was the Revolutionary war   True, he was not as distinguished an orator as he was a theologian   He had a fine presence, standing six feet in height, and was the personification of dignity   In fact, it is said that when Washington visited Newport, and Hopkins acted as Chaplain for the day   the figure of the theologian as he walked beside the great general was no less imposing than that of the distinguished visitor. But Dr Hopkins was not graceful, and had curious and awkward gestures   Dr. Channing has said that his voice was like a cracked bell, but probably Channing remembered the Hopkins of his later years when he was feeble or after he had suffered from a stroke   The children seemed to have been afraid of him, and one of them, a little girl who cried because she feared to go into the church, explained her distress thus: "When I look up into the pulpit, I think I see God there"   But in spite of his dignified demeanor, Hopkins had one of the warmest hearts that ever beat

The real curse in his speaking was his literary style, he knew his own weaknesses and regretted them, but ventured the explanation that since youth he had been more intent upon the discovery of truth than upon its expression And his explanation is probably true. Few men who are felicitous in their utterances know what they are talking about; those who know what they are talking about seldom can express themselves. Moses had insight enough to draw up a code of laws for Israel, but when he wanted to communicate with his people, he had to use the voice of Aaron. When Moses left

Aaron in charge of affairs, the people of Israel were persuaded by him to build a golden calf Herein is the tragedy of the thinker who cannot speak, and the speaker who cannot think.

It has been wrongly claimed that all Hopkins's sermons were metaphysical and abstract. Some of them undoubtedly were. But not all He was practical, and if he alienated many of his congregation from the church, it was not on account of his heretical theology but rather because of his attacks on the slave trade, to which we shall refer later. He took his preaching office most seriously. His sermon was always completed by nine o'clock Friday night. He spent Saturday in prayer and communion with God, and he went into the pulpit on Sunday directly from his private devotions Many of his sermons have been printed, and that which would most appeal to his audience is his "Farewell to the World," delivered in 1801, and being his last sermon in Newport. After considering the state of the world in general including the Mohammedans and the Jews, he turned to the church and its several branches, Greek, Roman and Protestant, and assured his hearers that only such as believed in the doctrines of John Calvin should be saved! Then he turned to the state of religion in New England, Rhode Island and Newport, and finally his own church and here again I crave your indulgence with a quotation .

"This town has long been noted for the many religious sects and denominations into which the inhabitants are divided, while the body of the people have been considered, I believe justly, to have very little true religion, if any; and they have appeared more dissolute, vicious, erroneous and ignorant, than people in general are in other parts of New England. And there has been no general revival of religion, or reformation, to this day, and the state and character of the inhabitants in general has not become better, but the contrary . .
A great part of them (Newporters) are so inattentive to religion, and so ignorant, that they

have really no religious principles; others have imbibed, and are strongly fixed in, religious maxims and notions, as contrary to the Bible as darkness is to the light   Of those who constantly attend public worship, including the professors of religion, very few of them maintain any family worship or religion and by far the greater part are so immoral in their conduct, or ignorant and erroneous in their notions of religion, as to fall vastly short of the Scripture character of true Christians   In this dark, unpleasant and melancholy view of the state and character of the body of the inhabitants of this town, I must take my leave, with a painful prospect of the evil which is coming upon them and their posterity, which they would not believe were they told. To most of them I cannot speak, and if I could, and they should know what I think and say of them, it would only serve to excite the resentment and indignation of the most."

To say the least, this is direct preaching, but it is not of a kind disposed to increase one's popularity!

But his great work was that of a theologian, and most of his writings were concerned with the justification of the strange ways of God with men   Into these writings we could not go if we would   But they furnished the material for the great theological arguments of the last half of the eighteenth century and the first half of the nineteenth   Hopkinsianism was a mighty system, a mixture of Calvinism and Arminianism.   It would not interest many of us today except those who study it for the history of theological thought. Nevertheless it once was vital and generally discussed. Among the names of the original subscribers to his System of Divinity are those of certain colored folk, to wit, Congo Jenkins and Zingo Stevens and Nimble Nightingale! Whether they read the books or not, is another matter.

The doctrines which distinguished this system from

orthodox Calvinism were those concerning the nature of holiness, and the reward of holiness Hopkins' idea was summed up in the phrase "disinterested benevolence." Sin, said Hopkins, is selfishness and to acquire holiness one must absolutely forget self; and think only in terms of the greatest good to Being in general We should live benevolently for God and for our fellow-men, with absolutely no anxiety concerning what joy or happiness our conduct would bring us in this life, or in the life to come. The true believer must do his duty and act for the glory of God He must be willing to do so, even if he be damned for it. His benevolence must be absolutely disinterested. A certain divine* has summed up the attitude of various theologies towards this matter as follows:

Calvinism "Love to God does not require in any one, under any circumstances, a willingness to be damned but the contrary."

Hopkinsianism. "No man truly loves God or his neighbor, who is not willing to be damned for a greater good than his personal salvation"

Universalism. "No man will be damned, and therefore no man should be willing to be damned."

Arminianism. "No man ever was willing, while in the exercise of love of God, to be accursed from him, for any cause"

Arianism. "No man who loves God can be willing to be damned for any cause."

Sabellianism. "Some say one thing and some another."

Socinianism "Love to God never can imply a willingness to be damned."

. *Deist.* "The Deists are so scriptural as to believe that no man ever hated his own flesh, and much less his soul, *if he has a soul.*"

All of which is very interesting We shall dismiss the theological system with these words, that his was a robust and heroic faith, and he himself was the incarnation of the theory of disinterested benevolence Much that is said

---

*Ezra Stiles Ely

against his theology is without any foundation, and he has been condemned for saying and holding theories he never held. But his doctrine of disinterested benevolence not only aroused the admiration of men like Channing and Whittier, but many liberal theologians declare today that his position was one of the most valuable contributions to theology ever made. It became common to put to all candidates for the Congregational ministry the query: "Are you willing to be damned for the glory of God?" until one of them in the middle of the last century broke the spell by answering: "No, I'm not, but I'm quite willing that the questioner be damned if it will serve God's glory."

I have purposely reserved what may be the most significant contribution of Samuel Hopkins until the last, and that is, his activity on behalf of the slave. In Great Barrington, as we have pointed out, Hopkins had observed the influence of the whites upon the Indians. But he had thought but little about the condition of the negroes. He owned a slave himself, who had been sold before he came to Newport. But he had not been in Newport long until he was forced to confront the slave trade in all its heinousness. Newport was one of the foremost slave markets, then and for many subsequent years. For instance, between the years 1804 and 1808, when Newport had declined, Rhode Island owned 59 of the slavers carrying negroes into Charleston, South Carolina. In that time, 17,048 slaves were brought into the port. Of these 6,238 came in boats owned in Rhode Island and 3,488, or more than one-fifth, in boats owned in Newport.* These figures will make the local situation very vivid. Hopkins saw the slaves in the slave market here, and he felt the inhumanity of this bargaining in human flesh. He decided to speak against the whole business, although practically no one had ever before lifted up his voice from a Christian pulpit with such a plea. He knew that he might arouse the antagonism of his parish, but with disinterested benevolence, he made his decision, and one Sunday morning he spoke his mind. As Whittier said "It well may be doubted, whether, on the Sabbath day, the angels of God, in their wide survey of his universe, looked upon a nobler

*Quoted in Park's Memoir.

spectacle than that of the minister of Newport, rising up before his slave-holding congregation, and demanding, in the name of the Highest, the 'deliverance of the captive, and the opening of prison doors to them that were bound.'" Whether his discourse was responsible for the measure or not, in June, 1774, the State of Rhode Island prohibited the further importation of slaves into this State.

But he did not stop with a sermon He wrote a dialogue which was published in 1776, the year of the war. He felt that at a time when these colonies were struggling for their own liberty, they would hearken more readily to an appeal for liberty on the part of those whom they themselves were oppressing While many were at the time opposed to the slave-trade and slave-holding, no "other man had prior to 1776 written on the theme so forcibly and fundamentally." This dialogue was afterward reprinted in 1785 by the New York Manumission Society of which John Jay was president and Alexander Hamilton a member, and was widely and powerfully used by the various abolition societies which were rapidly springing up. Hopkins was made an honorary member of this society, and also of the society of which Benjamin Franklin was president Not only did he preach against the slave-trade, but he succeeded in 1784 in having his church vote as follows "That the slave trade and the slavery of the Africans as it has taken place among us is a gross violation of the righteousness and benevolence which are so much inculcated in the gospel, and therefore we will not tolerate it in this church." True the Quakers had adopted similar views before, but the action of the First Congregational Church is a most significant item in the progress of the anti-slavery movement He also used the press freely, furnishing anti-slavery items to the editor of the Newport Mercury who, with fear and trembling and in face of the threats of his slave-holding subscribers, put as many as he dared into his paper. He wrote to Moses Brown, to the English abolitionists, and tirelessly and wisely he labored for this great cause. He is one of the great pioneers in the abolition movement, and Newport should be proud of him.

But he was no mere sentimentalist. He realized just

what the continuance of the traffick would mean He feared
that it might lead some time to Civil war, and he says so in a
letter dated 1788   He also recognized the fact that the task
of assimilating the blacks would be a great one, and consequently he proposed the formation of colonies on the Guinea
coast where blacks who had been cruelly torn from their
native land by the traders might be returned after having
enjoyed some of the civilizing influences of this country.
The scheme was partly missionary, and on that score
aroused the fear of his theological opponents who thought
it might be better to leave the Africans in their paganism,
rather than convert them to the Hopkinsian theology, but
it was far more than missionary in its nature.   It was put
forth with a statesmanlike understanding of the situation
as the following paragraph from one of his statements will
make clear:

> "This appears to be the best and only plan
> to make the blacks among us in the most agree-
> able situation for themselves and to render
> them most useful to their brethren in Africa, by
> civilizing them and teaching them how to culti-
> vate their lands and spreading the knowledge
> of the Christian religion among them.   The
> whites are so habituated by education and cus-
> tom to look upon and treat the blacks as an
> inferior class of beings, and they are so low by
> their situation and the treatment they receive
> from us that they never can be raised to an
> equality with the whites and enjoy all the
> liberty and rights to which they have a just
> claim, or have all the encouragements and mo-
> tives to make improvements of every kind,
> which are desirable   But if they were removed
> to Africa this evil would cease and they would
> enjoy all desirable equality and liberty, and
> live in a climate which is peculiarly suitable to
> their constitution   And they would be under
> advantages to set an example of industry and
> the best manner of cultivating the land, of

civil life, of morality and religion, which would tend to gain the attention of the inhabitants of that country and persuade them to receive instruction and embrace the gospel.

. . .These United States are able to be at the expense of prosecuting such a plan, at which these hints are some of the outlines. And is not this the best way that can be taken to compensate the blacks both in America and in Africa for the injuries they have received by the slave trade and slavery; and that which righteousness and benevolence must dictate? And even selfishness will be pleased with such a plan as this, and excite to exertion to carry it into effect, when the advantages of it to the public and to individuals are well considered and realized. This will gradually draw off all the blacks in New England, and even in the Middle and Southern states as fast as they can be set free, by which this nation shall be delivered from that which, in the view of every discerning man, is a great calamity and inconsistent with the good of society; and is now really a great injury to most of the white inhabitants, especially in the southern states." (1793).

Hopkins did not have good luck with his ventures, although he did raise funds to train two colored men for work in Africa. They were old men when they sailed and they both died within six months of their arrival in Sierra Leone. Though his scheme came to naught, must we not say that Dr. Hopkins was far ahead of his day, and had his advice been taken, America might have been saved the horror of the civil war, and the unsolved negro problem of today?

It should also be added that in forming the society to raise funds for the education of colored men intending to go to Africa as missionaries, Samuel Hopkins founded what is probably the first foreign missionary society in America, antedating the American Board by 43 years, as Rev. T. C. Mc-

Clellan some years ago pointed out. This, surely, is additional reason for attaching significance to the work of Samuel Hopkins

Such a man was Samuel Hopkins, preacher, theologian and reformer, who for more than thirty-three years claimed Newport as his home. He may have lacked a sense of humour, and some portions of his theology may make impossible reading, but history has few more radiant examples of disinterested benevolence. Systematic in his thought, he was systematic in his life. He rose at four every morning and studied until breakfast; then, after making the necessary purchases, retired to his study, where he spent most of the day and evening until nine o'clock, when he had family prayers: and at ten he went to bed. Modest concerning himself and his own powers, almost despondent in his humility, nevertheless he was as a defenced city against those who tried to make breaches in his theology or championed unrighteousness His life is a glorious example of the consecration and endurance of which the Puritan spirit was capable, and of which this nation may ever be proud and shall ever stand in need As Newporters, we should know more of him, seek to preserve the edifices associated with his name, and above all retain in our devotion to high ideals of piety and service, something of his incomparable spirit As the gentle-souled Whittier once wrote:

> " We need, methinks, the prophet-hero still
> Saints true of life, and martyrs strong of will,
> To tread the land, even now, as Xavier trod
> The streets of Goa, barefoot, with his bell
> Proclaiming freedom in the name of God
> And startling tyrants with the fear of hell.
> Soft words, smooth prophecies, are doubtless well
> But to rebuke the age's popular crime,
> We need the souls of fire, the hearts of that
>   old time."*

---

*"Men of Old "

Very Rev.
Dean George Berkeley, D.D.

A Paper read before the Newport Historical Society
March 6th, 1917

By
REV. STANLEY C. HUGHES

BISHOP BERKELEY

Among the eminent divines who elevated and enriched greater influence on his friends and contemporaries, or posesses greater charm for the reader of today, than George Berkeley; Doctor in Divinity, Dignitary of the English Church, Wit, Philosopher, Poet and Missionary He landed on our shores in January, 1729, covered with laurels won in the old world and burning with enthusiasm for a high enterprise to be carried forward in the new. He departed, sailing from Boston in the autumn of 1731, a disappointed and a broken man, his plans thwarted and his hopes dashed to the ground.

Of the man himself, the figure he made in the world, the philanthropic enterprise he cherished and which led him to come to America, his life in Newport and the causes of his failure and retirement to his native land, I will try to tell you in a few paragraphs, necessarily somewhat fragmentary. For those who care to know more, an ample supply of information coupled with entertainment and edification will be found in the four volumes of his life and works by Alexander Campbell Frazer, one of the best of biographers.

George Berkeley, son of William, an English royalist, was born in Ireland at Kilcrin, near Thomastown on March 12th, 1684 He was sent first to the famous Kilkenny School, founded by His Grace the Duke of Ormonde, where also Dean Swift and Thomas Prior were pupils, and then to Trinity College, Dublin. The troubled reigns of the Stuarts were drawing to a close. England was full of turmoil Many cavalier families, like those of Swift and Berkeley, had taken refuge in Ireland; and academic instruction was perhaps never on a higher plane than in those days Though an Irish school, I fancy, is never a poor place for the sharpening of the wits An Irish friend of mine was classmate in such a school of the late Father Tyrrell, author of "Christianity at the Cross Roads." He tells how they were one day construing Latin. Tyrrell came to the word "penna;" he translated it "wings." "Wrong," said the master "The word is singular number, a wing." "Oh!" said Tyrrell, "that is merely a difference of a pinion."

The Provost of Trinity College when Berkeley matriculated in 1700 was Dr Peter Browne, a prominent writer on Philosophic themes. His tutor was Dr John Hall, a learned and diligent teacher Twenty miles away lived Swift, at Laracor, whence he was transferred to be Dean of St Patrick's in 1713. In 1705 Berkeley and a group of his friends formed a Society to study the philosophy of Boyle, Newton and Locke. Among its rules was one that the conference begin at three in the afternoon on Friday and continue till eight Another ran. Whoever leaves the assembly before it's broken up, pay threepence. Evidently these young philosophers were bound to get at the bottom of things

In 1709 Berkeley was ordained Deacon and published his first philosophic work A second work appeared in 1710. In 1712, aged 28, he went to London; where he was presented at Court by his friend, Dean Swift, the following year and instantly won popularity and distinction both by his conversation and his published works It is said that he was so greatly in demand for week-end parties at country houses that he was once entrapped and compelled by main force to stay over Sunday. He was a friend of Steele and a frequent contributor to the Guardian; and on the first night of Addison's Cato he was with the author in his box. Pope's friendly description of him was "To Berkeley every virtue under heaven." Rarely, I suppose, has there lived a man before whom the paths of worldly success and ecclesiastical promotion stood more widely open What was it, then, that proved so attractive in this American Cathay as to draw him away from his assured fifty years of Europe at its best? What did he promise himself as the reward of so much sacrifice? It was the hope of founding a college in the Summer or Bermuda Islands for the education of the youth of the various American colonies, a Christian college in which priests and prophets of the Church might be raised up who should in turn go out into the wilderness and promulgate the Christian faith among the savages of the Continent. Berkeley was not blind to the vices of his age. He saw

through the veneer of fashionable society and was appalled
by the corruption that lay underneath   He knew the Court
well and was often sent for to hold theological debates with
Dr Clarke for the edification of the Queen. He had travelled
over the Continent and in Rome also   His deliberate conviction was that Europe was utterly debased and the only
hope for a pure and upright society lay in the unspoiled
people of the new world   It was this sentiment which
inspired his familiar verse:

> The muse disgusted at our age and clime
>   Barren of every glorious theme
> In distant lands now waits a better time
>   Producing subjects worthy fame
>
> In happy climes, the seat of innocence,
>   Where nature guides and virtue rules
> Where men shall not impose for truth and sense
>   The pedantry of courts and schools,
>
> Not such as Europe breeds in her decay .
>   Such as she bred when fresh and young.
> When heavenly flame did animate her clay,
>   By future poets shall be sung
>
> Westward the course of empire takes its way,
>   The four first acts already past
> A fifth shall close the drama with the day,
>   Time's noblest offspring is the last

The thought of reforming education for the good of
mankind has always charmed and fascinated men of great
character and intellect. Berkeley was obsessed by it for
years before he came to America   In 1723 he wrote: "It is
now about ten months since I have determined to spend the
residue of my days in Bermuda, where, I trust in Providence,
I may be the mean instrument of doing great good to mankind."   How quickly the fire of his enthusiasm caught in
other breasts may be judged from a letter of Dean Swift to
Lord Cartaret September 3, 1724: "There is a gentleman of
this kingdom just gone for England. It is Dr. George Berkeley, Dean of Derry, the best preferment among us. .   .
he is an absolute philosopher in regard to money, titles and
power; and for three years past has been struck with the
notion of founding a university at Bermudas, by a charter

from the Crown   He has seduced several of the hopefuliest
young clergymen and others here .   all in the fairest way
of preferment, but in England his conquests are greater and
I doubt will spread very far this winter . . . . His heart
will break if his Deanery be not taken from him and left to
your excellency's disposal "   Cartaret was Lord Lieutenant
of Ireland.

Armed with this letter of introduction to the Lord Lieutenant and with many powerful friends already enlisted in
his favor, Berkeley set out for London to launch his project.

A few sentences may be quoted from his printed Proposal by way of making clear the design he had at heart.
"Although there are several excellent persons of the Church
of England whose good intentions have not been wanting to
propagate the Gospel in foreign parts, who have even combined into societies for that very purpose . . . . it is nevertheless acknowledged that there is at this day but little
sense of religion and a most notorious corruption of manners
in the English Colonies settled on the Continent of America,
and the Islands   It is also acknowledged that the Gospel
hath hitherto made but a very inconsiderable progress
among the neighboring Americans who still continue in
much the same ignorance and barbarism in which we found
them above a hundred years ago. .   . . for the remedy of
these evils it should seem the proper method to provide, in
the first place, a constant supply of worthy clergymen for
the English churches, and, in the second place, a like constant supply of zealous missionaries well fitted for propa-
gating Christianity among the savages. . . Now the clergy
sent over to America have proved, too many of them, very
meanly qualified. both in learning and morals for the
discharge of their office   . . . These considerations make
it evident that a College or Seminary in those parts is very
much wanted; and   the providing such a Seminary is
earnestly proposed and recommended to all those who have
it in their power to contribute to so good a work."

The Proposal goes on to discuss the proper situation for
the College and fixes on the Island of Bermuda for a number
of reasons   First· for its excellent climate. Second· because
it is remote from the mainland with its temptations and

distractions. Third, for the reason that it is readily accessible from all parts of America, and can thus draw both whites and savages from the various colonies.

To us, today, Bermuda may seem too remote. But we must remember that when Berkeley gave his mind to the study of the situation, America was a strip of colonies lying along the Atlantic seaboard. There was nothing back of it. All commerce and intercourse was necessarily by water. It was not till 1776, the year in which Adam Smith's Wealth of Nations appeared, that James Watts constructed the first steam engine at Birmingham. Our continent is now covered with railways, then as undreamed of as automobiles or æroplanes. Had the College been built and endowed, supplied with food from the farm lands of Newport which Berkeley purchased for that purpose, and had steam locomotion not been discovered, there is no good reason why it might not have proved, if not all that its originator dreamed, yet one of the most beneficent Christian enterprises ever established in the Colonies. With twentieth century America stretching over the continent we feel the Bermuda scheme impracticable. So, no doubt, did a great many in Berkeley's own day. But such was the young Irishman's earnestness and eloquence, such his complete absorption in his generous and philanthropic enterprise, that he bore down all opposition and won the moral and financial support even of the indifferent and hostile.

He had come by a small private fortune in a most extraordinary fashion. On one occasion Dean Swift took him to dine with Mrs Vanhomrigh, whose daughter Esther was the Vanessa referred to in Swift's Journal to Stella. It seems probable that the lady never saw him again. But when she died, in the year 1723, it was found that she had left him the sum of £4000 in her will. With this assured capital in hand, sent, it seemed, by Providence, he felt himself ready to enter on his great work and began to solicit subscriptions and to besiege the Court for a charter for the College of St Paul in Bermuda. An incident in his campaign is related by Warton. Lord Bathurst told him that all the members of the Scriblers' Club being met at his house at dinner, they agreed to rally Berkeley, who was also his guest, on his scheme at Bermudas Berkeley having listened to all the lively things they had to say, begged to be heard in his turn; and displayed his plan with such astonishing and animating force of eloquence and enthusiasm, that they were struck dumb and after some pause rose up all together with earnestness exclaiming—"Let us all set out with him immediately." Nor was the zest transient. He persuaded many to help him More than five thousand pounds was raised—a large sum for those days—which might have been largely increased if the author of the Proposal had continued to rely on the good will of private persons.

By some means he won the ear of George I and the consent, if not the approval, of Sir Robert Walpole, the Prime Minister, then all powerful, whose name appears in the list of subscribers opposite the sum of £200. A royal charter was soon forthcoming, and with it a grant of £20,000 from the sale of lands in the newly ceded island of St. Christophers, approved by the House of Commons.

When one remembers the low estate of religion in England in the 18th Century, such a conquest of the Court and Court circles can be regarded as little less than miraculous. These were the days when favorites were promoted to high places in the Church as in the State; when Rectors, Deans, Prebendaries and even Bishops drew their salaries while never or rarely visiting their sees or parishs; when earnest men like Whitfield and Wesley and Fox were driven to find spiritual nourishment outside the Church, not willingly, but reluctantly, in very desperation Even the most sincere and religious seem to have looked on the set services of the Church as rather cold formalities The Earl of Egmont, for example, a stout supporter of the Church and a warm friend of Berkeley, has this to tell of a religious service, in his memoirs. "Sunday, Feb. 27, 1732 After dinner I went to the Kings' Chapel where I expected to meet the Bishop of Salisbury, brother to the Archbishop of Dublin, and resolved to show my resentment at the usage given Dean Berkeley. Dean Berkeley went to the chapel and sat over against us. I said to the Bishop: 'Yonder is one of the worthiest, most learned men in the three kingdoms who has met with the wretchedest usage ever was heard of.'" Then follows a long debate and a rather warm one between the Earl and the Bishop "This discourse between us," he adds, "was while the lessons were reading" Even the King's custom of sleeping through the services was not much worse than this

Thackeray has pictured the depraved court of George II in imperishable prose "Show me some good person about that Court, find me among these selfish courtiers, these dissolute, gay people some one being that I can love and regard. There is that strutting little Sultan, George II, there is that humpbacked, beetle-browed Lord Chesterfield; there is John Hervey with his deadly smile and ghastly painted face—I hate them. There is Hoadley, cringing from one bishopric to another, yonder comes little Mr Pope from Twickenham, with his friend the Irish Dean, in his new cassock, bowing, too, but with rage flashing from under his bushy eyebrows and scorn and hate quivering in his smile

I read that Lady Yarmouth sold a bishopric to a clergyman for £5000. Was he the only prelate of his time led up by such hands for consecration? As I peep into George II's St James I see crowds of cassocks rustling up the back stairs of the ladies of the Court; stealthy clergy slipping purses into their laps; that Godless old King yawning under his canopy in the Chapel Royal as the Chaplain before him is discoursing Discoursing about what? About righteousness and judgment. Whilst the Chaplain is preaching, the King is chattering in German almost as loud as the preacher. . . No wonder the clergy were corrupt and indifferent amongst this indifference and corruption. No wonder that skeptics multiplied and morals degenerated—I say I am scared as I look round at this society—at this king, at these courtiers, at these politicians, at these Bishops."

Surely it is an amazing and a cheering spectacle to turn from this picture to the mild and gentle priest in his seclusion on the Island of Peace, praying and studying and spending his fortune in good works and waiting so patiently for the promised grant that never came to erect his college for the instruction of American youth in the word of God and the training of priests who should go forth to convert the native tribes to the Christian religion.

And while we are quoting Thackeray it may not be amiss to add a few lines of his about Walpole, the accomplished, cynical Prime Minister, who presided over this corrupt Court and ruled England; the man to whom poor Berkeley must look for the payment of his grant. "In religion," says Thackeray, "he was little less than a heathen, cracked ribald jokes at big-wigs and bishops and laughed at High Church and Low   In private life the old pagan revelled in the lowest pleasures   He passed his Sundays tippling at Richmond; and his holidays bawling after dogs or boozing at Houghton with boors over beef and punch. He cared for letters no more than his master did"

Such was the group from which the zeal and devotion of Berkeley wrested a reluctant but substantial support for his enthusiastic scheme for the conversion of the blacks and savages of the New World; such the life on which he turned his back, rejecting its rewards and favors for the arduous toil of the missionary and the pioneer, not unlike Moses who esteemed the reproaches of Christ greater riches than the treasures of Egypt.

In 1727, June 14, King George I died   Strangely enough this scarcely halted the plan of St Paul's College On July 6 Berkeley writes to his friend Prior. "Dear Tom This is to inform you that I have obtained a new warrant for a grant, signed by His present Majesty, contrary to the expectations of my friends. who thought nothing could be expected of that kind in this great hurry of business."

All went well and on September 5th, 1728, the Dean sent his farewells to the same correspondent

"Dear Tom: Tomorrow, with God's blessing, I set sail for Rhode Island with my wife and a friend of hers, my Lady Handcock's daughter, who bears us company.   I am married since I saw you to Miss Forster, daughter of the late Chief Justice, whose humor and turn of mind pleases me beyond anything I know in her whole sex   Mr James, Mr Dalton and Mr Smibert go with us on this voyage. We are now all together at Gravesend."

The voyage must have occupied more than four months Our next information is derived from the invaluable Memoir of Henry Bull as published in the Newport, R. I., Republican Jan. 3, 1832—Dec 26, 1838 and Newport Mercury Jan 14, 1854—Nov. 23, 1861, Vol. II p. 119

Dean Berkeley's Arrival in Newport.[+]

This year, 1729, Dean Berkeley arrived in Newport, a notice of which we extract from the New England Weekly Journal, printed in Boston on Monday. Feb. 3rd. 1729.

"Yesterday arrived here Dean Berkeley of Londery in a pretty large ship. He is a gentleman of middle stature, of an agreeable, pleasant and erect aspect. He was ushered into the town with a great number of gentlemen, to whom he behaved himself after a very complaisant manner. It is said he proposes to tarry here with his family about three months"

What follows seems to be added by Henry Bull

Having undertaken the wild scheme of establishing a College in the Bermuda Islands for the conversion of the American savages to Christianity, aided by the promised patronage of the King and many of the influential clergy of the nation, he, with some others who followed his fortunes, sailed from England for the Island of Bermuda After a tedious passage they found themselves, as they supposed, in the latitude of the Islands but were not able to discover them, and after cruising about for some time in the neighborhood gave over the pursuit; they then concluded to return to England, and steering a northern course, tradition says they made land and hove out a signal, uncertain what land it was, but supposing themselves on the coast of America, and some part inhabited by Indians only. A boat came alongside of the ship in which was two of the Islanders, who informed them that the land in view was Block Island. They then inquired if they were in any of the English colonies of New England, and being answered in the affirmative they further inquired if there was any harbor and seaport town near, and were answered that a town called Newport

---

[+]Letter from Newport dated Jan. 24, 1729.

lay about thirty miles distant, where was an Episcopal church, the Rector of which was the Rev. James Honeyman. They then started for Newport, accompanied by the two Block Islanders who carried the ship into the west passage, the wind being adverse for entering the harbor of Newport The ship cast anchor between the Island of Conanicut and Narragansett The two men from Block Island landed on Conanicut and called upon a Mr. Gardner and Mr. Martin, both of whom were members of Mr Honeyman's church, and informed them that a great dignitary of the church from England—called Dean! was on board the ship, together with other passengers. They also produced a letter from the Dean directed to the Rev. Mr Honeyman, on the receipt of which Gardner and Martin came to Newport in a small boat to bring the intelligence and also to bring the letter—when on their arrival they found that Mr Honeyman was at the church, it being the day on which Divine service was held there, they then sent the letter by a servant, who delivered it to Mr Honeyman in his pulpit; he opened the letter and read it to the congregation, from the contents of which it appeared that the Dean might be expected to arrive every moment The church was then dismissed with the blessing and the Rev. Mr. Honeyman, together with Wardens, Vestry, church and congregation, male and female, repaired immediately to the Ferry Wharf, where they arrived a little before the ferry boat which contained the Dean, his family and friends The Dean was received on his landing by the gentlemen of the church and others of the town, who had collected thus hastily on the occasion, with the most respectful and hearty welcome; and the people, forming themselves in procession, escorted the Dean and his suite to the house of Mr Honeyman.

"The Dean continued about two years in Newport and often performed Divine service at Trinity Church. He purchased a farm about three miles from the compact part of the town, and built a house there, which he named White Hall and after his return to England in 1733 he presented the church with a fine organ

"What is contained in the preceding quotations was related to the writer by an elderly intelligent gentleman who states that it is according to his recollection of frequent conversations held at his father's house when he was about 14 or 15 years of age,by his father and Messrs Wickham, Malbone, Pease, Rev Dr. Eyers, Bisset and Gardner Thurston."

This entertaining and circumstantial account, the only one we have of the Dean's arrival, seems to err in one or two particulars. In the first place, as we have seen, the ship set sail for Newport and was by no means lost when she sighted Block Island, but close to her desired haven. In the second place, the picturesque detail of the Rev. Dr. Honeyman, wardens, vestry, church and congregation repairing to Ferry Wharf cannot be taken at its face value The day was Thursday, January 23, not a holy day in the church calendar and not the day on which Divine service was held That day was Sunday, and the distinguished visitor, as was quite proper, preached at the service on the Sunday following, from the text The Law and the Prophets were until John, since then the King of God is preached. St. L. 16:16. What probably happened was that the Rector was at church for a baptism or a wedding or some special service, got word of the ship's arrival, and informed some of his neighbors who went with him to the waterside.

However this may be the hospitable rector received the visitor and his wife into his home and entertained them for some months or until land had been bought and the Dean's house, his first home, for he had lived in college rooms, lodgings and the like all his life, was built Like a loyal cavalier he called it White Hall; and with every evidence of comfort and satisfaction he set up his lares and penates and enjoyed quiet domestic life; giving himself to study; and receiving, though rarely paying, visits.

Berkeley's accounts of Newport, written home to England, were, as is well known, most enthusiastic. He says he was never more agreeably surprised than at the sight of the town and harbour of Newport Again he described it as exhibiting "some of the softest rural and grandest ocean scenery in the world" He purposely set his house in a valley out of sight of the sea so that he might daily renew the fresh surprise of catching sight of the lovely shore.

"To enjoy what is to be seen from the hill," he said, "I must visit it only occasionally If the prospect were constantly in view it would lose its charm "

It was in July or August, 1729, that he removed from Newport to his farm and took up his residence. His three friends James, Dalton and Smibert removed at the same time from Newport to Boston. Here he lived the life of a studious recluse He never visited Boston till the day he sailed thence for England; and made no figure in the social life of Newport Now and then he paid visits to the Indians of the mainland in whose conversion he was deeply interested It is thus impossible to extract very much local color from his correspondence The passage from the memoirs of his grandson, Monck Berkeley, is well known As it was written by the Dean's daughter-in-law it may be regarded as authentic, in a sense, but it lacked the ring of versimilitude. "In one thing the various sectaries at Newport, both men and women, all agreed—in a rage for finery, to the great amusement of Berkeley, two learned, elegant friends, Sir John James and Richard Dalton, Esq, the men in flaming scarlet coats and waistcoats, laced and fringed with brightest glaring yellow. The sly Quakers, not venturing on these charming coats and waistcoats, yet loving finery, figured away with plate on their sideboards One, to the no small diversion of Berkeley, sent to England and had made on purpose, a noble large tea-pot of solid gold, and inquired of the Dean, when drinking tea with him whether Friend Berkeley had ever seen such a curious thing. On being told that silver ones were much in use in England but that he had never seen a gold one, Ebenezer replied, "Aye, that was the thing. I was resolved to have something finer than anybody else They say that the Queen has not got one " The Dean delighted his ridiculous host by assuring him that this was an unique; and very happy it made him."

But if he did not mingle very much with the gay fashionable red and yellow-coated society of the day, the Dean managed to draw round himself two circles not less interesting to his mind: a conference of clergymen which occasionally met at his house, and the famous Philosophical Society out of which sprung the Redwood Library. "The missionaries from the English Society, who resided within a hundred miles of Newport," writes Mrs Berkeley, the Dean's wife, "agreed among themselves to hold a sort of Synod there twice in a year, in order to enjoy the advantages of his advice and exhortation. Four of these meetings were accordingly held. One of the principal points which he then pressed upon his fellow laborers was the absolute necessity of conciliating by all innocent means the affection of their hearers, and also of their dissenting neighbors." No record of the meetings of this conference has been kept. But the letters that passed between Berkeley and the most distinguished of the American participants in the discussions, Samuel Johnson, are deeply interesting and form an important link in the chain of American Philosophic thought.

"Johnson was born at Guildford, Conn., of a family prominent in the Congregational Church. He graduated from Yale College in 1714 and was tutor there fro m1716-1719. By reading the works of eminent Anglican divines—I quote Prof Frazer—and after many conferences among themselves, Cutler, then Rector of Yale College, Johnson and some other ministers, were led, about 1722 to doubt the validity of Presbyterian ordination and the expediency of extempore common-prayer. They soon announced their new convictions and cast in their lot with the Church of Hooker, Cudworth and Barrow . . . . Cutler, Johnson and Brown now resigned their pastoral charges in the neighborhood in order to connect themselves with this communion. In 1722 they crossed the ocean to obtain Episcopal ordination in England. Johnson is said to have visited Pope at his villa, who gave him cuttings from his Twickenham willow. These he carried from the banks of the Thames and planted on the banks of his own beautiful river at Stratford, in Connecticut, when he was settled there in 1723." It seems that Johnson, a very scholarly and thoughtful man, had fallen in with Berkeley's earlier works and had been by them converted to his Idealistic Philosophy. Upon Berkeley's settling in his vicinity he naturally sought the opportunity for frequent conference. A warm acquaintance sprung up and a copious correspondence ensued on various philosophic subjects. The reader who is curious to understand Berkeley's philosophy, and it is one of the the world's great systems, cannot do better than read Alciphron, that charming Dialogue almost as clear and limpid in style as one of Plato's own, written here at Newport while its author sat in his chair near the Second Beach, gazing out over the ocean, and then turn to the letters between Berkeley and Johnson in which minute points are gone over at length. Take this sentence, for example, pitched upon almost by chance — "You say you agree with me that there is nothing within your mind but God and other spirits, with the attributes or properties belonging to them and the ideas contained in them." Berkeley to Johnson, The master is setting his pupil's feet on the assured ground of a common agreement. To know anything is to perform an intellectual or mental process. To be knowable, then, all things must be, in a degree, of the same texture as the mind. As we study Nature and learn her ways we follow an intellectual path always. And the one great mind that holds all things in its grasp, and has made them knowable by us is God. When Berkeley looked on the scenery of this perfect pearl of an island he thrilled with a sense of pleasure almost beyond words to express because, I suppose, its beauty seemed to him to reflect visibly the grace of God. That connection is the key that unlocks the secret of the loveliness of Nature Wordsworth came upon it as a little lad when he thrashed the hazel coppice for nuts and then, having gotten his hazelnuts, stood aghast to see how the shattered trees seemed to utter a mute protest to Heaven

> And unless I now
> Confound my present feelings with the past
> Ere from the mutilated bower I turned,
> Exulting, rich beyond the wealth of kings,
> I felt a sense of pain when I beheld
> The silent trees, and saw the intruding sky—
> Then dearest Maiden, move along these shades
> In gentleness of heart, with gentle hand
> Touch—for there is a spirit in the woods

Johnson learned this great truth, the secret of the highest poetry and the highest philosophy, from Berkeley. He himself later published a book "Elementa Philosophica," printed by Benjamin Franklin at Philadelphia in 1752 He was the founder of King's College, now Columbia University, in New York.

Members of the Philosophic Society were Col Updike, Judge Scott—a grand-uncle of Sir Walter Scott—Nathaniel Kay, Henry Collins, Nathan Townsend, the Reverend James Honeyman and the Reverend Jeremiah Condy. Johnson of Stratford and McSparran, Church of England Missionary in the Narragansett country, occasionally attended the meeetings.

Two children were born to the Berkeleys in Newport. The first was a boy, Henry by name The Church Register gives the record of his baptism "1729 September 1st, Henry Berkeley, son of Dean Berkeley, baptized by his father and received into the Church " The second was a daughter who died in infancy, and whose grave is near that of Nathaniel Kay in the church yard

Two strains of sadness and anxiety run through the Newport letters. His friends had begun to wonder at his delay in departing for Bermuda It seemed to betoken uncertainty; and subscriptions were no longer forthcoming. As a matter of fact there was no sort of use in leaving Newport till the royal grant should be paid, for he had spent his private fortune in buying the White Hall farm and had nothing to go on with But this was the second trouble, the money from the Exchequer was not forthcoming The royal and noble personages who had favored it and the politicians who had voted it had not the slightest interest, naturally, in the savages or their religion. They had been interested in and won over by the towering genius and enthusiasm of Berkeley He being gone their interest died. From the moment he sailed away from England there had ceased to be any likelihood whatever that a penny of the St. Christopher money would every follow him. So here in Newport he waited and worried and ate his heart out and wrote letters to all his friends begging them to intercede with the Government for him. The incident furnishes an excellent commentary on the text. Put not your trust in Princes. December 23rd, 1730, Lord Percival wrote to say that Walpole had finally confessed that the money would never be paid; one of those statements politicians can make in private but must resist and repel the accusation of in public. Already the unhappy truth had forced itself home on poor Berkeley's mind Hope deferred had made his heart sick He wrote from Newport: "As for the raillery of European wits I should not mind it if I saw my college go on and prosper, but I must own the disappointments I have met with in this particular have nearly touched me, not without affecting my health and spirits." This, with another in the same tenour were the last letters he wrote from America In the Autumn of 1731 he sadly set sail from Boston On Friday, February 18th we find him preaching the annual sermon before the Society for the Propagation of the Gospel in Foreign Parts in the Church of St. Mary-le-Bow.

"Rhode Island," he tells his hearers, "is inhabited by an English Colony consisting chiefly of sectaries of many different denominations who seem to have worn off part of that prejudice which they inherited from their ancestors against the National Church . , though it must be acknowledged at the same time that too many have worn off a serious sense of all religion, . being equally careless of outward worship and of inward principles. The native Indians have been debauched by the whites with strong drink," adding, "it would seem that the likeliest step towards converting the heathen would be to begin with the English planters . To conclude if we proportioned our zeal to the importance of things; if we would love men whose opinions we do not approve; if we knew the world more and liked it less; if we had a due sense of the Divine perfections and our own defects, and if, in order and all this that were done in places of education which cannot be done so well out of them—I say, if these steps were taken at home while proper measures are carrying on abroad the one would very much facilitate the other."

From which it appears that, while he had given over his hope of elevating the education of the Colonies he had not in the least changed his mind as to the propriety or necessity of doing it

It is to be regretted that we have no extended notice of

the Dean's preaching in Newport nor one of his sermons entire, only the rough notes of twelve of the discourses. It would be interesting to know what the colonists thought of the preaching of one who was regarded as a model of eloquence in his own land. Personally they liked him and were delighted to have so distinguished a neighbor and flocked to the church to hear him. But whether they approved his rhetoric or contrasted it unfavorably with that of their native preachers, as seems not unlikely, does not appear.

As for the sermons themselves they are notable in two respects. In the first place the earlier sermons are very general in their nature and very conciliatory in tone. One for example, evidently fitted to the minds of dissenters, begins thus. Divisions into essentials and circumstantials in Religion. Circumstantials of less value (1) from the nature of things, (2) from their being left undefined; (3) from the concession of our Church which is foully misrepresented. Sad that religion which requires us to love, should become the cause of our hating one another."

But, second, as time wore on and the preacher became better acquainted with his environment, studied the society about him and formed a definite impression of its deepest religious needs the tone changes. Very frankly, as a good physician of the soul, he puts his finger on the sore spot in the community. One can scarcely believe these later sermons were as popular as the first. I quote the account of them given by Moses Coit Tyler in his volume. Three Men of Letters p 41. "Two of the most notable of his American sermons are significant of his penetrating study into the characteristic vices of a community neither sensual or frivolous, vices born of the ungenerous activity of a legion of unbridled tongues. These sermons furnish us with examples of his aptitude for social criticism—criticism so finely edged as to culminate into something like satire. "Vices, like weeds, different in different countries; national vice familiar, intemperate lust in Italy; drinking in Germany; tares wherever there is good seed; though not sensual, not less deadly. e g detraction; would not steal sixpence, but rob a man of his reputation; they who have no relish for wine have itching ears for scandal; this vice often observed in sober people; praise and blame natural justice; where we know a man lives in habitual sin unrepented, we may prevent hypocrites from doing evil; but to judge without inquiry to show a facility in believing and a readiness to report evil of one's neighbor; frequency, little horror great guilt."

Satan "tempts men to sensuality, but he is in his own nature malicious and malignant, pride and ill-nature, two vices most severely rebuked by our Saviour   All deviations sinful, but those upon dry purpose more so; malignity of spirit like an ulcer in the nobler parts; age cures sensual vices, this grows with age; imposing on others and even on themselves as religion and a zeal for God's service, when it really proceeds only from ill-will to man and is no part of our duty to God, but directly contrary to it."   These extracts while not indicating the literary style of the Dean's preaching at least show us something of his way of thinking.   They show also that he agreed with St. James as to the relative value of sins of the tongue.

Whitehall and his library he conveyed to Yale College, a very generous gift.   Later he sent an organ and a bell to Trinity Church where he was long remembered.

He kissed hands for the Diocese of Cloyne, January 17th 1734, a position which he held till 1752 when he retired to Oxford, residing on Holywell Street   Here, on the evening of Sunday, January 14th, he passed away, surrounded by his family.   His wife had been reading aloud to the little family party the lesson in the Burial Service taken from the 15th Chapter of the 1 Ep. to the Corinthians, and he had been making remarks on that sublime passage.   His daughter soon after went to offer him some tea   She found him, as it seemed, asleep, but his body was already cold, for it was the last sleep—the mystery of death, and the world of the senses had suddenly ceased to be a medium of intercourse between his spirit and those who remained.

The Sephardic Jews of Newport

A Paper read before the Newport Historical Society
June 12th, 1917

By

REV. J. PEREIRA MENDES, D.D.

Ministers of the Earlier or Sephardic Jews of Newport

What is the meaning of the word "Sephardic"?

Who were, and who are, the Sephardic Jews?

In what way are they different from any other Jews?

And above all, what have they accomplished in human history for humanity's uplift?

History is written by the finger of God.

Sometimes man attempts to write a chapter for his own gain or glory. Then paragraphs are written with blood, or pages are blurred with tears, or deceit can be read between the lines. But just as the battlefield, scarred, stained and burnt, becomes in time by the magic of God, covered by growths which hide and beautify, so the aftermath of human sin is the mercy and pardon of God, evidencing that "God has passed by."† The contests and sufferings which history records, the sorrows and horrors born of man's inhumanity to man, are by the chemistry of God made to lead to better conditions which hide and beautify the unsightly past. By some Divine alchemy they are made to produce a re-creation. By some Divine miracle they are transmuted into what stands for Human Happiness and makes for Human Progress

In this magic and mercy of God, in this chemistry, alchemy, miracle of God for Human Happiness, Progress and Uplift, the Sephardic Jews, like all other Jews, have been humble instruments of the Divine Will. Their special work in human history I shall presently indicate

To show how human history as written by man is overwritten by the finger or hand of God, let me illustrate by citing but one or two striking instances from ancient, medieval and modern history.

---

† This expression means Divine forgiveness of human sin. It is used in Exodus, xxxiv · 6, in the passage describing how some of the Hebrews were seduced to worship Apis, the calf, one of the gods of Egypt, by the Egyptians who left Egypt with them. Their disloyalty brought due punishment, but "He passed by" and mercifully and graciously forgave.

Babylon wrote her conquest of Jerusalem and the "Seventy Years' Captivity" to proclaim the triumph of Babylon But the hand of God overwrote or re-wrote it to declare the triumph of God, for it tells of the purification of our nation, its preparation for its world-task of spreading the kingdom of God westward in and beyond Judea. And was it mere coincidence or was it the finger of God, that just in that very era, when Jewish thought was felt in Babylon, the then metropolis of the world where those great Jewish schools of learning were origined, the three greatest thought-leaders, Zoroaster, Gotama Buddha and Confucius carried Eastward lofty thoughts of Hebrew tinge?* Four centuries later Syria meant her conquest of Palestine to write Syria's glory But the finger of God re-wrote it, to mean the victory of Monotheism, achieved by Judas Maccabeus, over Polytheism, a victory which alone made possible the births of the daughter-faiths, Christianity and Islam which have done so much to lift mankind from classic mists and desert myths to a clearer conception of the One "God Universal," to whom Abraham, first of the Hebrews, built his early altar† and of whom Malachi, last of the prophets, spake.‡

Xerxes wrote history to proclaim Persia's ambition to orientalize Europe But the finger of God rewrote it to mean the rescue of Europe forever from Orientalism, thus to make possible Human Progress and Civilization upon which Human Happiness rests

In what we may call medieval history, Pope Hildebrand and William the Conqueror wrote the Conquest of England to spell subjugation of peoples' rights and the increase of Papal power The Pope even gave the Norman a ring as if to mean the marriage of Church and State. But the finger of God re-wrote that chapter of English history to spell Runnymede, or the triumph of the peoples' rights, to mean Wyclif, and presently Cranmer and Henry, through

---

*The victory of good over evil, an era of world-peace, filial reverence are Hebrew concepts adopted by Zoroastriaism, Buddhism, Confucianism respectively

†Genesis XXI. 33.

‡Have we not all one father—hath not one God created us? Malachi II · 10

whom England was divorced from the Papacy, not married
to it, to mean the eternal divorce of Church and State, and
freedom of the people, freedom of conscience, "now and
forever!"

And who doubts but that the history of today now
being written with blood and blurred with tears, will, by
God's magic or alchemy, by the finger or hand of God, be re-
written to mean man's democratization, to mean human institutions and conditions that shall mean human betterment
and uplift, secured by a peace with honor for all nations,
that shall be a Peace Permanent   The Sephardic Jews have
been elements in this chemistry or alchemy of God   The
history of the Sephardic Jews has been written by man, but
it has been, time and time again, re-written by the hand of
God   .

When Rome conquered Jerusalem and long lines of cap-
tives left Palestine for the galleys, the mines and amphi-
theatres of their Roman masters, Rome wrote a page of her
history designed to tell of Roman glory   But the hand of
God rewrote that page, to mean the salvation of mankind
from the coming dark and middle ages, eras of which no
Roman even dreamed or could dream.

The Sephardic Jews are those who settled in Spain,
called Sepharad, and on the Mediterranean coast.   The
term "Sephardic Jews" is now applied to their descendants.

Hebrews had for ages before the destruction of Jerusalem, * or the Christian era, been settling in many a city
of the Roman world.   The prophet Joel tells of Hebrews
sold as slaves to Greece. †   The historic books speak of the
trade of Tarshish, identified with ancient Tartessus.   Rojas
states that five hundred years before the **Christian era, He-**
brews built Toledo or Toledoth, Escaluna, Magueda, Cada-
holsa, Guardia, Romeria, Almoroz, Noves, Nombleca and the
present Tembleque in Spain   Marianna connects the advent of the Jews in Spain with the era of Nebuchadnezzar.
De Leon remarks in his preface to the history of the Jews
of Bayonne that it is said that a synagogue existed at Toledo

*The year 70 of the common era

†Joel IV · 6

before the destruction of the Second Temple. De Leon also speaks of a number of Jews carried with their families to Spain after the destruction of the First Temple

Some of these families assumed to be descended from the royal house of David, and alleged that their ancestors had been established from time immemorial in and around Lucena, Toledo and Seville. Graetz mentions these traditions and the derivation of the names of several Spanish towns from Hebrew words, such as, Toledo from Toledoth, Escaluna from Ascalon. etc That Hebrews were in Spain long before the Christian era is also indicated by a letter written by the Jews in Spain declaring that they had no part in the Crucifixion as they were then in Spain. Some may say these are mere traditions But tradition is the echo of history hovering over the hills of time

Certainly the numbers of the Hebrews in Spain were vastly swollen by the advent of their unfortunate brethren driven forth by the legions of Titus and later by those of Hadrian after the Bar-Cochba rebellion was crushed They were known as Sephardim, because Sepharad, mentioned by the prophet Obadiah is identified with Spain

Certain it is that the term Sephardim is taken to mean the Hebrews around the whole Mediterranean coast, easterly up to Babylon and the Euphrates, overspreading westerly into south France, and after the expulsion from Spain in 1492 in all directions,—into Holland, the Turkish Empire, North, Central and South America, the West Indies, Kingston, Ja , and Surinam; Newport and New Amsterdam being among the chief settlements in the Northern part of this Hemisphere.

The history of the Sephardim, thanks to the hand of man, shows tear-stains and blood-marks to mankind's eternal shame

But thanks to the hand of God as He re-wrote it, we find that the historic work of the Sephardic Jews has been wonderfully blessed, for it has meant the blessing of humanity, in as much as it helped to preserve science, to cooperate with the Arabs for the presentation of much of the learning of the classic world, and to prepare men's minds for the tremendous event in human history, the Reformation In other words, the Sephardic Jews helped to uphold the banner of learning, to proclaim liberty of conscience, to promote the consciousness of man's personal accountability to God and thus to forward mankind's centuried march toward true civilization and happiness

How this came about may now be briefly told

When Goths and Vandals conquered Spain, on the Fall of the Roman Empire, they found Jews already settled in the country

At the end of the Sixth century, when the Roman Catholic form of Christianity became the recognized religion of Gothic Spain, persecution of the Jews began, driving many to the neighboring shores of North Africa

There they came in contact with the Moors, who in 711, under Tarik, invaded Spain to avenge the outrage of his daughter by a Spanish potentate.

In five years the Moors conquered Spain, and the glorious era of the Jews in Spain began.

In the year, 750, Abd-er-Rahman ruled; he founded the University of Cordova, the schools of Seville, Lucena, Granada, encouraged Jewish and Arab scholarship whose exponents and professors received students from all parts of the world Numerous Jews attained high honor and lasting fame as poets, philosophers, astronomers, physicians, mathematicians, grammarians, lexicographers, financiers and merchants Through their linguistic skill, they translated classic authors from Latin or Greek into Arabic, while at the same time they gave Eastern lore to the Western world. Withal, they united the study of the Scriptures and traditional learning, combining intense mental activity with social and domestic culture

The Arabs had sedulously collected and translated the Greek philosophers, but not the Greek poets because they abominated the lewdness of the gods of Olympus and abhorred the idea that any God could be guilty of such licentiousness as displayed in an Iliad or Odyssey. To every mosque was attached a school, education of the young being considered essential It was the dawn of a wonderful revival of learning in that most remote corner of Europe, in the very era of European history known as the dark and middle ages

Was it chance, or was it the hand of God, that while in those sad days of darkness, ignorance, bloodshed, crime, priestly incompetence and immorality throughout Europe the lamps of learning, idealism, morality were lit in far-off Spain by the Arabs and those Sephardic Jews?

Note the hand of God preparing things from far-off times, and then see the part in the Divine plan for mankind's weal performed by those Sephardic Jews in Spain

The story can be rapidly outlined.

Alexander the Great carried Greek language, Greek philosophy, Greek art, Greek science into the East, about 330.

Justinian closed the schools in Athens in 529 But the hand of God nevertheless continued and fostered their work in Syria. For the teachings of those schools or what we term "Greek learning" lived on. And before those teachings could die out, the Abassid dynasty of Mohammedan came into power (750) and encouraged the translation of Greek learning into Syriac and Arabic. That meant their perpetuation of those teachings. Hippocrates and Galen in medicine, Euclid, Archimedes and Ptolemy in mathematics and astronomy; Aristotle, Theophrastus and Alexander of Aphrodisias in philosophy, were so translated and carried by the Arabs into Spain There they and the Sephardic Jews introduced this learning into Christian Europe through the famous universities and schools of the Arab and Sephardic-Jewish professors in Spain, and presently in South France, Italy and Sicily and even Egypt, for those seats of learning were thronged by students from all parts of Europe who carried back to their distant homes, the thought-seeds there planted in their minds.

The philosophical renaissance in Latin Europe was due to the introduction of translations of Aristotle's works

The learned fathers of the Christian Church, the scholastics, imbibed much of their wisdom from distinctly Jewish writers Albertus Magnus, Vincent of Beauvais, Thomas Aquinas used Afer's translation of the philosophy of Isaac ben Solomon Israeli, the Arab-Jew of Egypt, (born c 855)

William of Auvergne, Albertus Magnus, Thomas Aquinas, Duns Scotus, Siger of Brabant studied the Mekor Hayim or Fons Vitae of Solomon, son of Yehudah Ibn Gabirol (1021-1070). The Spanish Jew, better known as Avicebron; Ibn Sina, more generally known as Avicenna; Ibn Roshd, better known as Averroes, Abraham ben Hiya better known as Savasorda, (a corruption of the Arabic title Sahib al Shorta), attest the influence of Sephardic Jewish thought on the Christian "intellectuals" of their day.

And deeply did Albertus Magnus, Alexander of Hales, William of Auvergne, (the Bishop of Paris) and Thomas Aquinas, study the monumental work known to us as the More Nebuchim or "Guide to the Perplexed," of the great Spanish-Jewish philosopher, Maimonides And who has not heard the familiar distich—"Si Lyrus non lyrasset, Lutherus non saltasset"—"If de Lyra had not played, Luther would not have danced."—indicating Sephardic "Jewish thought-influence on the Reformation-movement,—a movement which their brethren, the Ashkenazic" or German Jews, promoted in no slight degree

We are told of writers on chronology, numismatics, oratory, agriculture, irrigation, botany, zoology, pharmacy, medicine, surgery, mathematics, both arithmetic and algebra, even quadratics, trigonometry, astronomy, in that remarkable era of the Arabs and Sephardic Jews in Spain. I repeat they were, under the hand of God, the preservers of the torch of learning in that remote corner of Europe just when Europe itself was in the dark and medieval ages.

Is it any wonder that when presently some of the descendants of these Jews of Spain found their way to Newport, they brought with them culture, enterprise, commerce?

Is it any wonder that all the world over, traces of this era of wonderful mentality are evident? Witness in our ordinary every-day language the many Arabic words introduced and commonly used, such as syrup, julep, elixir, admiral, alchemy, alcohol, algebra, chemise, cotton, cipher, carat, zenith, the names of stars on astronomical charts, all are Arabic. Their pupils and co-workers, the Sephardim, carried them wherever they went, even as they carried culture, enterprise and commerce

Those Arabs and Jews taught geography from globes! They used the pendulum, the astrolabe, the mariner's compass. They made maritime discovery easier.

From Barcelona and other ports, an immense trade was carried on, mainly by Jewish energy In the days of this prosperity a thousand ships, we are told, carried trade to far-off Constantinople and the Black Sea. What wonder then, that they brought commerce to Newport when they came—what wonder that that Newport prince-merchant, Aaron Lopez, had such a fleet of shipping, as I shall presently illustrate!

In those days of the Sephardic golden age, the streets of Cordova were paved and lighted with lamps, though Paris and London had only mud-paths, with an occasional lantern, or no light at all. Learned professors threaded the streets of Toledo and Seville while footpads made London streets dangerous in those tenth, eleventh and twelfth and even later centuries.

Houses or homes in England and France were cheerless; often a hole in the roof was the chimney and rushes or grass served for carpet—or there were worse conditions, a cranny for chimney, bare earth for carpet!

In Moorish Spain, houses stood in wonderful courtyards, hot and cold water pipes were introduced, and even pipes to convey perfume from flower-beds into boudoirs or banquet rooms combined refinement with pleasure and convenience

Music and poetry were cultivated. Some of the music we have It is plaintive, sweet, moving

The type of Hebrew poetry of the age bespeaks nobility of mind, lofty thought, independence of reason, reverence for God

As the Christian power gained and the Moorish power waned, the condition of the Jews changed for the worse The very prosperity of the Jews begot extravagance and disloyalty.

But, as always in Jewish history, Jewish disloyalty meant Jewish suffering.

Persecutions began. Vincent Ferrer, a Dominican Friar, Marcus Rodrigues, Halorqui of Lerea, an apostate, were storm-petrels, who by their preachings presaged the tempest.

In 1473 all Andalusia or South Spain, was deluged with Jewish blood

In 1481 the Inquisition was established under Torquemada. In his eighteen years of office, 10,220 Jews were burnt alive; 6,860 were burnt in effigy, 97,321 were condemned to perpetual imprisonment, confiscation, etc.

On March 31, 1492 the full fury of the tempest burst. The decree was published that all the Jews were to be expelled from Spain.

On August 30, the law was enforced and Spain expelled her best brains

Thus man wrote the record.

But the finger of God wrote something else.

For on that same April 30, Columbus was ordered to equip his fleet to sail Westward

On August 2nd, the Jewish exiles left Spain

On August 3rd, Columbus sailed, with him at least five Jews, de Torres as interpreter, and four mariners, to discover a land destined to mean the aggrandizement of humanity by American Ideals, American Energy and American Enterprise and Invention

In all of these, the Sephardim Jews have played a worthy part in the history of America. But the finger of God has written more, as we have now discovered

For as Prof Adams remarks, "Not jewels, but Jews, were the real financial basis of the first expedition of Columbus" That is, it is not true that Queen Isabella sold her jewels to finance Columbus. He was financed by two Jews, Luis de Santangel, Comptroller at one time of the State of Arragon, and Sanchez of Saragossa.

Of these Sephardim exiles many went to Portugal, only to be driven out in a few years; to South France, to Holland where they helped "Brave Little Holland" to free herself from Spain's domination and the Duke of Alva's cruelty, and to Turkey where Sultan Bajazet received them remarking how strange he thought it that a King should expel such desirable subjects!

Many of the French refugees migrated to the West Indies, and some to Newport and New Amsterdam

Many from Portugal went to Brazil, and when Brazil was captured by the Portuguese from the Dutch, they also came to Newport and New Amsterdam.

Many from Holland went to New Amsterdam, that being a Dutch settlement. Now Turkish refugees have begun to come here, but only in the last score of years. There are probably 25,000 in America. Ten years ago there were not 500. Many speak the old Spanish of 1492; some speak Greek and some speak Arabic as their home language. They are descendants of those Sephardic or Spanish Jews who, when expelled from Spain in 1492, found refuge in Turkey, as I stated a moment ago.

In the spring of 1658, says Peterson in his history of Rhode Island, "Mordecai Campanal and Moses Packeckoe (or Pacheco) arrived in Newport with fifteen others. It is said they introduced Free Masonry, (three degrees)

The spirit of Roger Williams assured them welcome, for he had said "I desire not that liberty to myself which I would not freely and impartially weigh out to all the consciences of the world besides All these Consciences, yea, the very Consciences of the Papists, Jews, etc. . . . ought freely and impartially to be permitted their several respective worships and what of maintaining them, they freely choose "

They increased in numbers, and in prosperity soon made headway because of their culture, strict integrity and respect for their religion.

Governor Cozzens on 20 May, 1863, in a public speech, said "Between 1750-1760 some hundreds of wealthy Israelites, a most distinguished class of merchants, removed here from Spain, Portugal, Jamaica and other places, and entered largely into business One of them, Mr. Aaron Lopez, owned a large fleet of vessels, rising 30 at one time in the foreign trade and many more in the coasting trade * The order-boxes or pigeon-holes, as we sometimes call them, with the names of his vessels upon them, are still to be seen in one of the old stores on the Lopez (now Finch and Engs) wharf " †

The manufacture of sperm-oil and candles ‡ was introduced into Newport by Jews from Lisbon 1745-50.

---

*A strange chance placed a quantity of Aaron Lopez's papers in my hands the day after this lecture. For "the largest fleet of vessels" see Note at end of this essay

†See Note.

‡See Note

In 1760, they had in Newport, seventeen factories for these; twenty-two distilleries, four sugar refineries, five rope-walks, many furniture factories supplying New York, West Indies, Surinam, etc

They certainly meant Energy, Enterprise and Invention in Newport, then a most important city, commercially.

In 1770, eighteen vessels arrived in one day from the West Indies. It is on record that on one occasion, the good citizens were awakened to further progressiveness, by being warned that New York might outstrip them!

The Lisbon earthquake in 1755 brought some accessions to the Jewish community

In that year, Ezra Stiles, well known today as a notable President of Yale, wrote to a friend in Birmingham, England, "There are fifteen Jewish families in Newport They have no minister." He must have been wrong about the number, for we know the names of many more   (See note in Appendix)

Three years later, the Rev Isaac Touro arrived from Jamaica to be the minister   He speedily quickened the spiritual life; for on the first of August, 1759, only one year after his arrival, the foundation of the synagogue was laid in Griffin Street, now Touro Street, and on Friday, the Second of December, 1763 it was dedicated. Many members of the sister-congregation in New York, of which I have the honor of being minister, journeyed from New York for the Consecration, some of them and the Congregation itself having contributed towards the cost of erection.

The Rev. Isaac Touro proved himself a faithful shepherd during his all too short pastorate. He was a learned Hebrew scholar. It was through him and later, through Rabbi Haim Isaac Carigal of Jerusalem, that the above-mentioned Rev Ezra Stiles, then Presbyterian Minister residing in Newport, derived his own Hebrew knowledge A close friendship existed between these three, and Dr. Stiles in his diary, frequently alludes to them, to his friendly relations with them, to visits to the synagogue, etc.

In 1775 he left for a visit to his native land   Probably the outbreak of the great war with England prevented an early return as intended Death intervened and prevented it forever. His two sons, Abraham and Judah, had been left in Newport, but on the outbreak of the war, were taken to Boston by their uncle, Moses Michael Hays. His piety, learning and modesty, his realization of his responsibilities as minister, his zeal in the promotion of the spiritual life of his flock, his close friendship with Christians of the standing of Dr. Stiles, combined with inherent culture which reflects the conditions of that Golden Age, the era of the Jews under Arabic auspices, gained for him general respect

It was by holding up these conditions of true citizenship, that the Sephardic Jews brought to this country, into its national as well as its commercial and social life, the elements which best secure a nation's prosperity and well-being. For with energy, enterprise, invention, industry and commercial ability, those early Sephardic Jews of Newport preached by life and example the three great, the three greatest, R's, "Reverence, Righteousness and Responsibility." Without these three "greatest" R's, no nation lives!

When the Revolutionary War broke out, to quote the Rev Frederick Denison who lectured on the Jews of Newport before the R. I Veterans Association, (Dec 7, 1885), "The Jews were friends of the Colonies in the Revolutionary struggle They gave liberally of their means to sustain the patriot cause In some cases they served in the continental armies "

One of the Lopez family is said to have exclaimed to the American recruiting sergeant who had rejected him because he was too old, "I am not too old to stop a British bullet!"

A member of my congregation in New York still has the original autograph letter of George Washington to the Jews of Newport, and I have a photographed copy in my study, acknowledging the loyalty of the Jews of Newport in the highest terms And other Jewish communities in other towns received similar acknowledgement.

Newport's commercial supremacy was ruined by the war. Aaron Lopez, the most prominent Jewish citizen, lost many a ship by British privateers. The family of Lopez, Riviera (cousin) A Pereira Mendes, (son-in-law) went to

Leicester, the Hays family to Boston; the Seixas family to New York. Their names are identified with the establishment of Free-Masonry in Rhode Island, the founding of the Redwood Library and the Leicester Academy; they contributed to Trinity chimes, they were honored with trusteeship of Long Wharf. Their record is a proud one. Not once did they figure in any court in any civic dispute. (See Appendix *). Not one indictment appears against them in court records.

The Jewish community dwindled away gradually. In 1818 but three were left and I have their pathetic letter to my congregation asking us to take charge of their sacred scrolls, thus making us the guardians of their affairs, as in deed we naturally would be, by common ancestry, history and traditions, besides kinship.

A few years later the Newport civic authorities wrote to our congregation in New York, as the Guardians, to repair the wall or fence of the Synagogue plot, which was done. I have the minutes of our congregational action recording this.

The Synagogue remained closed for many years, the building and the burial ground sustained by munificent bequests of the brothers, Abraham and Judah Touro, sons of the former minister, the Rev. Isaac Touro - (See Appendix VI)

On the 20th December, 1882, the Trustees of the Synagogue in New York extended a call to my honored father, the Rev. A. Pereira Mendes, Head of a Collegiate Institution in London and acting Ecclesiastical Chief of the Sephardic Jews of that city, to take the spiritual charge of a few Jews who had recently settled in Newport. Their action was taken in response to the City Council's referring those new settlers who wished to use the old building, to the New York Congregation.

The new minister duly arrived, and maintained the high ideals of the old settlers. He established the traditional Ritual which he rendered with all its dignity and charm, winning to it the new settlers, whose ritual, Hebrew pronunciation, melodies and customs were different, being Ashkenszic not Sephardic.

Of naturally scholarly instincts, he became known to

Newport leaders of scholarly culture. He lectured for the general Newport public on Jewish subjects, such as "The Talmud"; for the Rhode Island Historical Society on "The Old Jewish Cemetery," transcribing and translating the old inscriptions from the Hebrew or Spanish or Portuguese or Latin into English, and he gave Hebrew instruction to any members of the Christian clergy who would go to him.

The new community grew but slowly

He passed away to his eternal sleep in 1893

His name, inscribed on a mural tablet in the Synagogue, attests the love and respect of the little community, but his name lives yet in the hearts of all who today remember his ministrations, his quiet geniality, his courtliness, his loyalty to the highest ideals of Jewish and civic culture, his life exposition of all that adorned the traditions of the Sephardic Jews of Newport and of the world.

This is the story of the Sephardic Jews. Summed up, it is a story of effort to carry out the ideals of God, to promote culture, to energize industry, but all on the lines of the three greatest R's, "Reverence, Righteousness and Responsibility"

And the two Sephardic Jewish ministers of the old Newport Synagogue, the Rev Isaac Touro and the Rev Abraham Pereira Mendes were true exemplars of the best Sephardic Jewish traditions.

NOTE—Aaron Lopez's ships In one bill alone of Aaron Lopez, dated 1765, rendered to him by Geo H Peckham, I find mentioned the Betty (sloop), Three Sallys (Sloop), Charlotte (brigantine), America (ship); Guineman (ship), in my papers, I have twenty-nine names on one slip, and several other lists in other memos.

NOTE—Finch and Engs Wharf. I was fortunate enough to obtain a bit of an old Lopez-desk some years ago when in Newport.

NOTE—The manufacture of candles. The beautiful candelabra in the Newport synagogue attest the number of candles used to illumine even one edifice

APPENDIX The will of Judah Touro is a marvel He left large sums of money to Christian as well as Jewish charitable institutions

Rev. GEORGE WHITEFIELD

A Paper read before the Newport Historical Society
January 2, 1917

By
Rev. WILLIAM I. WARD

George Whitefield in Newport

Within a comparatively recent period of time the attention of the American people has been freshly called to the English clergyman, George Whitefield, who, by reason of his evangelistic impulse, impassioned eloquence and unremitting zeal, was, a century and a half ago, at the zenith of a remarkable career as a Christian preacher. Just a few years ago Charles Silvester Horne, a justly famed preacher of London, delivered at Yale University, on the Lyman Beecher foundation, an illuminating course of lectures to which he gave the title, "The Romance of Preaching" In one of the lectures he spoke at length of Mr Whitefield as a notable exemplar of the passion of evangelism and said of him that it is he "who as pointedly raises, for the student of oratory and its permanent effect, the problem of emotional preaching" To the large number of Americans who heard these lectures, and to the larger number who have read them, Mr. Horne described Mr. Whitefield as a preacher "facing the multitudes under God's sky, with the heavens for a sounding board, the hillside for a meeting house, and some rude boulder for a pulpit"; and as having a "splendid energy expressing itself in the fold and sweep of his robes, and a passion for souls in his kindled countenance, his flashing eye, and the tender solemn tones of his voice"

Shortly after these lectures had been delivered and published the two hundredth anniversary of the birth of George Whitefield occurred. This was in December, 1914. At different places in our country, and in various ways, the anniversary was observed and attention called to the fact that, during a period of thirty years, he was an active factor in the religious history of America as well as of England. He visited all the American colonies, from New Hampshire to Georgia. Twice he came to Newport. This fact is our justification for making extended reference to him under the auspices of this Historical Society.

Because of his great religious fervor, his intense missionary zeal, his extraordinary powers of oratory and his
marked evangelistic ardor Mr Whitefield became conspicu-
ous among the illustrious Christian preachers of the world.
As a result of his distinguished devotion to his calling and
of his prodigious labors in his native land and also in this
new world, to which he opened his heart widely, the people
of our tongue on both sides of the Atlantic gave him earnest
and responsive hearing. He was an ordained minister of
the Church of England. With the Wesleys and several
others he shared membership in the Holy Club of Oxford,
and he was thoroughly sympathetic with its spirit of warm
personal devotion and eager religious activity Thus he
helped earn the derisive title "Methodist" and was justly
classed with those who first bore the title. We may as well
add that he helped, not a little, to win honor for the title.
He did not, however, accept the Arminian type of theology.
Holding in this respect with the Calvinists he had distinct
affiliation with that body of dissenters who believed and
taught the tenets of the Genevan scholar Thus it is seen
that he had belongings with several bodies of religious leaders, and so it may be argued that he was too large a per-
sonality to be bound to any one of such bodies or, on the
other hand, that he was too indefinite in his thinking to ally
himself with either one of them Certainly the facts prove
that no one of them can lay exclusive claim to him.

George Whitefield was born in the English city of Gloucester, at the Bell Inn, in Southgate street, in the month of
December, 1714 His father, who was the keeper of the tavern,
died about two years later. His mother, who continued to
keep the inn, was careful about his education and sought
to keep him from too close contact with the tavern business.
Nevertheless he gave her, for a year or two, after he had
passed his fifteenth year, considerable assistance in the care
of the house Already he had spent three years in the
grammar school conducted by a church in the city Here
he had developed a thirst for knowledge and so much interest in dramatic studies, as well as talent in this direction,
that the master of the school chose him to make the annual
speech before the corporation of the city. A little later he

entered Pembroke College, Oxford, earning his way for a part of the time by working as a servant in the College. While he was there his most intimate fellowships were with the more religious members of the university. When he was but twenty-one years of age, two years earlier than was customarily allowed by the church, he was ordained a deacon, in his native city of Gloucester, by Bishop Benson who, two years or more later, ordained him to the priesthood at Oxford It is said that the Bishop, becoming displeased because of some of Whitefield's activities, expressed regret that he had ordained him; but that he subsequently took a different view of the matter and, "when upon his death bed, sent for Whitefield, besought him to remember him in his prayers and gave him money for the support of his work"

Through the influence of the Wesleys Mr Whitefield became interested in the colony of Georgia He collected funds for the support of the colony and he made his first voyage across the Atlantic to visit it. Noticing many needy orphans in Georgia he established an asylum for them and carried their cause very close to his heart until the end of his life. This trip to America was repeated six times and as often as he came he zealously endeavored to do good Since he was primarily an evangelist his chief work was to quicken, by his earnest and persuasive preaching, the religious and spiritual life of the people.

But there are other abiding marks of his helpful influence in this country. He gave assistance to Harvard College, aiding in replenishing its library after it was burned in 1764. He gave encouragement to the Indian school at Lebanon, New Hampshire, which afterward became Dartmouth College, raised money for it and interested his friend, Lord Dartmouth in it. He secured funds in Scotland with which to help establish Princeton College and he gave help to the University of Pennsylvania in its early stages

From his seventh and last trip to America he did not return. The days of this visit were destined to be his closing days upon earth and he was soon to find, here in New England, the resting place for his body.

It was during his second visit to America that Mr. Whitefield was invited to come to New England. Respond-

ing to the invitation he seems to have made Newport his
port of entry He arrived here in September, 1740, passing,
after a brief stay, to Boston and to other points farther north,
thence westward to Northampton, Massachusetts, and then
to New Haven, Connecticut.

Newport became aware of the approach of the stirring
evangelistic preacher. News preceded him as to the criticisms which were made upon his public ministrations, criticisms such as no preacher of his type has ever escaped
One of the churches of the town, the Second Congregationalist, whose location was that of the present place of worship of the Second Baptist Church, thought it wise to declare
itself in advance of his coming. It therefore passed a formal vote saying "that as Reverend George Whitefield is expected in town speedily, and as his preaching in many other
places has caused great contentions and divisions in many
churches, this meeting house be shut against said Whitefield,
and he be not suffered to preach in it " This was not, however, the unanimous or the prevailing sentiment with reference to the distinguishd visitor. The pastor of the First
Congregational Church, the Reverend Nathaniel Clapp,
greeted him cordially and went with him to call upon the
Reverend James Honeyman, rector of Trinity Church. Mr.
Honeyman granted the use of this church for a two days'
meeting. Twice on each of these days, morning and afternoon, the people crowded into the church to listen, and
after the close of the last service a thousand persons followed the preacher to his lodgings where he stood at the
door and preached to them on "hungering and thirsting after
righteousness."

It seems very likely that Mr. Whitefield was readily admitted to the pulpit of Trinity Church by reason of the fact that
he had been fully ordained in the Church of England. And
when we remember that the Second Congregational Church
had been organized because of strong dissatisfaction with
Mr. Clapp's administration as pastor of the First Church, it
seems not impossible that Mr. Clapp's courtesy to Mr. Whitefield may have been stimulated, to some extent, by the action of the Second Church Certainly the large audience
which gathered to hear the preacher showed that the people

of Newport were fully as responsive to his eloquent oratory as those in other places.

It was thirty years later when the famous preacher was in Newport for the second time. Dr. Samuel Hopkins, who became pastor of the First Congregational Church in 1770, having heard him preach in New Haven, was pleased with him and approved him. On the third day of August, four months after his installation, he received Mr. Whitefield as guest in his home, the parsonage on Division Street. At five o'clock in the afternoon of the next day the noted evangelist preached in Dr Hopkins' meeting house on Mill Street to an audience which crowded the building, using the text "Take not thy holy spirit from me." It is reported that a young Jewess who heard him at this time greatly admired his preaching of the gospel of Christ. The following day was Sunday. In the morning he preached for Dr. Ezra Stiles, in the church whose doors had been closed against him at the time of his earlier visit. His text at this time was "Acquaint now thyself with God and be at peace." At six o'clock in the evening he preached in the field close by Dr. Hopkins' meeting house using as a text "Other foundation can no man lay than that is laid which is Jesus Christ." A company of from one thousand to fifteen hundred persons listened to this sermon. Dr Edwards A. Park, from whose "Memoir of Samuel Hopkins," we glean many of the facts here recited, says, referring to this occasion, "He stood while preaching on a table which is still reverently preserved." Two days later he preached at five o'clock in the afternoon in the Baptist meeting house where Mr. Thurston was minister. Thirteen hundred people were said to have been within the building to listen while four or five hundred more stood outside. On the next morning, at six o'clock, he preached once more in the First Congregational Church taking the second verse of the first chapter of Genesis as his text.

Dr. William Patten, who was at a later period, pastor of the Second Congregational Church and who wrote a little book on the life of Dr. Hopkins, gives an account of Mr Whitefield's second visit in Newport, which varies slightly from the one found in the larger book written by Dr Park.

He states that the preaching in the field occurred on the morning of the Sabbath instead of in the late afternoon Since Dr. Park gives the story of the whole day and writes, upon the whole, with greater fulness of circumstances, it seems probable that his statement is the correct one. But some of Dr Patten's comments are very interesting. Speaking of the preacher he says "A gentleman present informed the writer that he exceeded any man he had ever heard in oratory and in representing to the life everything of which he spoke. Though he stood upon a table he appeared by his movements and gestures to be in no want of room When he read the psalm appeared new to him and he could scarcely believe he had ever read or seen it When he prayed it was in accents so earnest and winning that he looked up to see if the Holy Spirit, whose presence he invoked, were not visible in the form of a dove" Evidently New England, proverbially cold and critical, was not unmoved by this fervent messenger of the gospel But this further comment is made "Except in cheering and exciting the saints there was little apparent spiritual benefit from these labors Many admired his oratory, his manner and his conversation; but only a few, if any, were brought under conviction of sin and to repentance." In the spirit of fairness the writer further remarks that it was characteristic of Newport to be slow in responding to any definite religious appeal

Dr. Patten further records that Dr. Hopkins said he was persuaded of Mr Whitefield's piety and eminent success in awakening sinners and bringing many to Christ, but that his early education and his itinerant manner of life as a preacher limited his opportunities for thorough investigation as to subjects of doctrinal and experimental religion Consequently he was not as consistent and instructive as he might otherwise have been; and, in his early ministry, he was sometimes rash in his censures, especially with reference to ministers who did not agree with him This fault in Mr Whitefield, which Dr. Hopkins pointed out so definitely is by no means uncommon Eager evangelists, even to our own day, have often exhibited this weakness

It is quite evident that Mr. Whitefield did not lack for

open hospitality when he made his second visit to our city
How general was the cordial feeling toward him was, perhaps, indicated by a social event which occurred on the last
day of his stay in Newport He dined that day at the home
of John Wanton, a member of the Society of Friends; and
with him were Drs Hopkins and Stiles, the Congregationalist ministers, Mr. Thurston, the Baptist preacher, and Mr.
Rusmeyer, the pastor of the Moravian congregation in Newport

We have noticed no reference to the Episcopal Church
or its rector in connection with Mr. Whitefield's second visit
If it be true, as might seem to be implied, that this church,
whose doors were promptly opened to him thirty years before, did not now publicly recognize him, it should be remembered that he had doubtless become during this period
of time, quite separated, in his public activities from the
church in which he had received his early training and ordination to the Christian ministry Much of his public work
had been done in connection with the dissenting bodies.
During the early part of the period he had been in close
sympathy with the Wesleys out of whose work grew the
largest of the non-conformist bodies, and he never ceased,
no matter how much he differed from them in some matters,
to agree with them as to their reasons for undertaking religious work independently of the Established Church of
England He had been one of the leaders in the doctrinal
controversy which resulted in the organization of one of
the smaller denominational churches in England and Wales
He had also become the head of an independent church in
London which, to this day, bears his name and is one of the
strongholds of English Congregationalism In view of the
intense feeling which was characteristic of doctrinal and ecclesiastical controversies at that period it is not strange if
the Church of England and her American daughter suffered
him to come and go unnoticed.

There is reason to believe that Mr. Whitefield's ministry
in Newport was not without some permanent influence
Some evidence to this effect is associated with the memory
of a woman who was, for many years, a notable person in
the religious life of the place, Mrs. Sarah Osborne. She

was a young woman when he made his first appearance here. In the published account of the earlier portion of her life, which was written by herself, she refers to him saying "In September, 1740, God in His mercy sent His dear servant Whitefield here." and it is recorded that his preaching greatly impressed her and led her to a deeper religious consecration Not long afterward she formed some of the women of the church into an organized body, which was later known as the "Osborne Society," for the cultivation of the religious life. A weekly devotional meeting was held; and one of its members was said to be so gifted in prayer that "she could pray for an hour and a half without in any way repeating herself and without anyone being weary.'

When Mr Whitefield was in Newport for the second time the American colonists were growing restless under what they held to be the oppression of the mother country and the time of revolt was drawing near It is interesting to know that Mr .Whitefield sympathized with the colonists and expressed his sympathy warmly although the movement which culminated in the war for American independence was but begun when he died When the storm of conflict broke Newport suffered greatly, indeed was almost ruined Nearly five hundred private dwelling houses were destroyed, Church buildings, with some well known exceptions, were torn down or seized for use by the English army. Drs. Hopkins and Stiles, pastors of the two Congregational Churches, both of whom spoke boldly and strongly in favor of independence, were virtually driven out of town Neither of their congregations could hold public worship or carry forward the usual activities of a Christian Church But Mrs. Osborne was still living and full of good works She had the respect of the British soldiers who spoke of her as "the good woman." Her home was among those which was spared destruction, and in that home was held the weekly prayer meeting of the society which she had organized, the only visible thread of life in the Congregational body during several troubled years Thus the influence of Mr. Whitefield's preaching may have had much to do with saving an important Christian organization from destruction at a very critical period in the life of our city.

Allusion has been made to the fact that Mr. Whitefield stood upon a table when he preached in the field near the First Congregational Church Of this table we may say now, as Dr. Park said many years ago, it "is still reverently preserved" It is now the property of the United Congregational Church to whom it was given by Dr. Thatcher Thayer some forty years after he came to Newport to become pastor of the Church. It is circular in form and is about three feet in diameter. The top is solid mahogany and is made in three sections Two of these sections are attached by hinges to the third and central part and they form leaves which may be turned down on the sides The top is supported by four curved legs two of which are so connected with the frame that they may be swung outwardly, one on either side, as supports for the leaves when they are extended The upper surface of the table has been smoothed and polished, but the under side is still somewhat rough A sheet of paper is attached to the under side of the table top, covered with glass which is framed with narrow moulding On the paper is the following inscription:

This table was given to me by Miss Philadelphia Ellery, toward the end of her life. It was given to her by her father, William Ellery, one of the signers of the Declaration of Independence, who stated to her that Whitefield preached standing upon it.

THATCHER THAYER

To Dr Thomas Wood

July, 1883

Dr Wood, to whom this note was addressed, was the clerk of the United Congregational Church at the time when the gift was made. William Ellery, one of whose descendants is now a resident of Newport, was a worshipper at the Second Church.

The table is not the only visible memorial in the city, of Mr. Whitefield. At least four buildings in which he spent some time are still standing. These are Trinity Church, the

Second Baptist Church, which was originally the Second Congregational Church, the building on Mill Street which was erected as a house of worship of the First Congregational Church but is now used for business purposes, and the house on Division Street, numbered forty-six, where Mr. Whitefield was the guest of Dr. Hopkins.

Rev. Dr. William Ellery Channing

A Paper read before the Newport Historical Society
April 3rd, 1917

By

Rev. WILLIAM SAFFORD JONES

WILLIAM ELLERY CHANNING

.

"And this green, favored island, so fresh and sea-blown,
  When she counts up the worthies her annals have known,
  Never waits for the pitiful gaugers of sect .
  To measure her love, and mete out her respect.

"Three shades at this moment seem walking her strand,
  Each with head halo-crowned, and with palms in his hand,—
  Wise Berkeley, grave Hopkins, and, smiling serene
  On prelate and puritan, Channing is seen

"One holy name bearing, no longer they need
  Credentials of party, and pass-words of creed
  The new song they sing hath a threefold accord,
  And they own one baptism, one faith, and one Lord!'"

Thus Whittier, in his poem on "The Quaker Alumni",
links together in one apostolic order of the spirit these three
lights of the world in their several generations, Berkeley,
Hopkins, and Channing, all of whom in one way or another
touched and moulded Newport life and thought. But Berkeley, though he profoundly impressed the community with
his philosophic acumen and spiritual consecration, was after
all more or less of a bird of passage; and Hopkins, though
for so many years "a son of thunder" in an easy-going, self-
satisfied community, was not born here and did not come
here till he was well on in middle age. Channing, however,
was a son of Newport, and the blood of several generations
of Rhode Islanders flowed in his veins Then, too, he never
lost connection with this fair isle. Even though his name
and fame are indissolubly bound up with the life and spirit
of Boston, we must remember that year after year for many
summers he returned with delight to this island of Aquidneck. Channing often fervently thanked God that he was
born on Rhode Island In his correspondence with Miss
Lucy Aiken, the niece of Mrs. Barbauld, he calls this the
most beautiful island in this country.

And Channing was grateful for birth in a State which treasured the "soul liberty" of Roger Williams and his ideal of "a free church in a free state". And the spiritual atmosphere into which he was born had been impregnated by the ideas of come-outers like Samuel Gorton and Anne Hutchinson and John Clarke. No wonder that Channing could say at the age of fifty that he was "always young for liberty".

Before the Revolution Newport was a more important seaport than New York. Its mail-bags were bigger. Southern planters came here to spend the summer, and though on pleasure bent were not averse to buying slaves from Africa, who were sold frequently on the wharves for rum or cash. These poor slaves while they were being auctioned off were crowded into cages. Then there were three hundred Jewish families in Newport, furnishing merchants and ship-owners in goodly numbers. Lopez, a Portuguese Jew, was the owner of eighty-eight square riggers, all in the foreign trade. In 1774 Newport boasted a population of nine thousand. It was larger than Providence. But the next year there were only five thousand in Newport. The Revolution hit it hard. Its foreign commerce was ruined. Its Golden Age was over. The British occupation was a terrible thing for the island. Hundreds of houses were burned. All the woods and trees on the island were cut down. The winter before Channing's birth, 1779-1780, was a time of bitter distress for the Newporters who opposed King George and supported the cause of the Colonies.

We gain a vivid idea of the Newport of that day by dipping into the journal of the Baron du Bourg and the letters of Comte de Rochambeau and the diary of Ezra Stiles. Dr. Stiles, who had been elected President of Yale College but had not yet formally severed his connection with the Second Congregational Church, came back to Newport on a pastoral visit in the spring of 1780. He describes his desecrated church and the well-nigh ruined community. While here he preached two Sundays, May 21st and 28th. He records in his Diary, Vol. II, page 426 "1780, May 28th Lord's Day. I preached to my flock A. M. Cant. II. 2-4, and administered the Lord's Supper to thirty-two communicants. P. M. I preached again, and baptized William Ellery Channing, son of the Hon. William Channing. Esq., Attorney General of the State of Rhode Island " This child, destined to be so famous, had been born on April 7th, in the house which is now fittingly enough, the Children's Home When Channing came into the world Lafayette was on the high seas, coming from France with the glorious news that a French fleet and army would soon be on the way to help secure the independence of the Colonies.

In his sermon delivered in Newport in 1836 at the dedication of Dr. Hopkins's church as a Unitarian Congregational house of worship, Channing paid this tribute to President Stiles, who baptized him: "Another noble friend of religious liberty [he had just spoken of the Rev. Mr Callender] threw a luster on this island immediately before the Revolution. I mean the Rev. Dr. Stiles, pastor of the Second Congregational Church, and afterwards President of Yale College. This country has not perhaps produced a more learned man. In his faith he was what was called a moderate Calvinist, but his heart was of no sect. He carried into his religion the spirit of liberty which then stirred the whole country He respected the right of private judgment, where others would have thought themselves authorized to restrain it . . He desired to heal the wounds of the divided Church of Christ, not by a common creed, but by the spirit of love. He wished to break every yoke, civil and ecclesiastical, from men's necks. To the influence of this distinguished man, in the circle in which I was brought up, I may owe in part the indignation which I feel towards every invasion of human rights. In my earliest years I regarded no human being with equal reverence I have his form before me at this moment almost as distinctly as if I had seen him yesterday. So strong is the impression made on the child through the moral affections."

When Dr Samuel Hopkins came back to Newport the very spring of Channing's birth, after the British occupation of three years, he found the rich people mostly gone, many houses burned (including his own), and his church, the First Congregational, so badly burned that it was unfit for use. But what troubled the good old man most of all was the moral and spiritual condition of the town. He found much immorality and indifference And the religious community was split up into little groups of Quakers, Baptists, Free-Will Baptists, Seventh-Day Baptists, Episcopalians, Moravians, Methodists, Universalists, Individualists of every peculiar kind But there was no union of these religious forces against scepticism, intemperance, and sensuality When, however, Hopkins entered the pulpit to denounce these evils and kindred iniquities like the traffic in African slaves and rum, it was said that "sinners trembled and good men rejoiced".

Channing always confessed a great debt of gratitude to Dr Hopkins He revered Dr Stiles, as we have seen, he also looked upon Dr. Hopkins as a father in Israel When Dr. Stiles went to Yale his congregation worshipped with Dr. Hopkins's for the first six years of Channing's life From Dr Hopkins, therefore, the boy Channing must have received his first instruction in the catechism, and that meant the Westminster As the Rev. Charles T. Brooks has said in his valuable "Centennial Memory of Channing"· "Grace was given the child to reject the indigestible shell of Calvinistic irrationalities and inconsistencies, and take only (what indeed, after all, the noble-souled old warrior valued more than all) the kernel of reverence for truth and honest conviction."

"The more important of Channing's recollections of Dr. Samuel Hopkins", says John White Chadwick, in his noble biography of Channing, "are those touching the relations of the two men in the younger's early manhood Those touching his first impressions were much less favorable But the slightest contact between two religious leaders who, differing widely, had still much in common, is too precious to be overlooked After Jonathan Edwards, with whom Hopkins enjoyed an affectionate intimacy, no one brought to New England Calvinism a more intellectual and spiritual interpretation. Some forty years ago Mrs. Stowe's 'Minister's Wooing' renewed this popular interest in his character and thought, with some violence to the facts affecting his domestic life. It has been his too exclusively known opinion that 'we should be willing to be damned for the glory of God'.

The fact that he was actually and very practically willing to be, and was, damned by many Newport gentlemen and traders, for his interference with their business of slave-catching and owning, has had scanter recognition."

When I think of Hopkins and Channing, I always think of that early winter morning when the boy looked from his window across the gardens between his home and the gam-brel-roofed parsonage, and saw the grand old man working away by candle-light on some kindling thought that prevented sulmber

William Ellery Channing was the third of ten children, only one of whom died in infancy. Three of the nine made a name for themselves in the world He came from the best stock, what Dr. Holmes would have called "the Brahmin caste of New England", being related to the Ellery, Gibbs, Dana, Allston, Cabot, Lee, Jackson, and Lowell families. The first American Channing was John Channing, who came from Dorsetshire, England, in 1711 Soon after his arrival in Boston he married Mary Antram, who had come over on the same ship with him Their son John was a Newport merchant who lost the fortune he had made. He married the widow Robinson, born Mary Chaloner. After her husband's death she kept a little shop for the support of her family Between customers she knitted vigorously, we are told Everyone respected her John Channing was the father of William Channing and the grandfather of William Ellery Channing William Channing, the father, was born in Newport, June 11, 1751 He was a graduate of Princeton in the class of 1769 He read law in Providence, began to practice here in 1771, and in 1773 married Lucy Ellery. He was a lawyer of marked ability, but rather too fond of politics for the good of his family He was at the same time attorney-general of the State and United States district-attorney He was a loyal son of Princeton and came near sending his boy, William Ellery, there. As Princeton theology has always been of a very different stamp from that of Harvard, we naturally speculate as to what might have happened if Channing had gone to Princeton instead of to Harvard. Would he have changed the spiritual atmosphere of Princeton or would it have changed him?

The elder Channing was deeply religious, and a strong supporter of the Congregational Church He took an active part in the restoration of Dr Hopkins's meeting-house His intercourse with Dr Stiles, his former minister, had broadened his mind. This liberality of opinion he passed on to his children. In a time and society much given to profanity he was entirely free from it. "I recollect with gratitude", says William, "the impression he made on my own mind I owed it to him, that, though living in the atmosphere of this vice, no profane word ever passed my lips " A genial man, occasionally his pent-up wrath would explode vigorously, as it did on one occasion when William was hearing his father plead a case in court. The boy was so frightened that he rushed from the court-house. When Rhode Island adopted the Federal Constitution of 1787, at the late date of May 29, 1790—she was the last of the original thirteen to come into the Union—young Channing was present at the convention with his father. It was a joyous day for both. The elder Channing hailed the French Revolution with enthusiasm, but the putting to death of Louis XVI was too much for his faith and hope Young William's grandfather, John Channing, the merchant, had owned slaves, but soon after the Revolution they were all freed. In their "bewildering freedom" the elder William was very considerate in his treatment of them. The boy was admitted to his father's office at choir practice every week,—a keen pleasure for him. The elder was a famous gardener, and not content with one garden must have two, to supply his friends' tables as well as his own. But though attached to his children, he was never intimate with them. The custom of the time made for a certain austerity and dignity, even in the family circle.

Channing's mother, Lucy Ellery, whom he resembled in feature, though not in expression, hers being hard and cold while his was mild and luminous, was the daughter of William Ellery, the signer of the Declaration of Independence. She was short in stature, as was her famous son. But what was said of her could have been said of him "She made the most of her inches by her erect carriage and elastic motion " William Henry Channing, the nephew of William

Ellery Channing and his biographer, speaks of her "rough nobleness", which I take to mean that she was in the habit of speaking her mind plainly, if not always calmly. We are told that a familiar household note was "Don't trouble yourself, Lucy; I will make all smooth." Thus her husband poured oil upon the angry waters But her son William idolized her, as we see from the following tribute: "The most remarkable trait in my mother's character was the rectitude and simplicity of her mind Perhaps I have never known her equal in this respect She was true in thought, word, and life. She had the firmness to see the truth, to speak it, to act upon it. She was direct in judgment and conversation, and in my long intercourse with her [she lived till he was past fifty] I cannot recall one word or action betraying the slightest insincerity She had keen insight into character. She was not to be imposed upon by others, and, what is rarer, she practiced no imposition upon her own mind. She saw things, persons, events, as they were, and spoke of them by their right names. Her partialities did not blind her, even to her children Her love was without illusion. She recognized, unerringly and with delight, fairness, honesty, genuine uprightness, and shrank as by instinct from everything specious, the fictitious in character, and plausible in manners." What a good description of Channing's own character!

But, says his biographer, Chadwick, "he was not a happy boy because his parents, doing their duty by him in the most conscientious manner, were not affable and friendly with him, gave him a stony formalism when he craved spontaneous affection, were of the opinion that he should be seen and not heard, and that he should know his place. Then, too, there was the burden of the inherited theology and the cheerless piety of the New England Puritan early to solemnize his tremulous heart." But let it not be inferred from this that he did not take part with the other boys in all their sports and games. He was very fond of roaming about on the wharves and climbing to the tops of the tallest masts His longing for a lofty outlook began early, you see. After attending four different dame-schools he went to the school kept by the famous Master Rogers, who trained the intellects and moulded the characters of many who afterwards became distinguished Washington Allston, who was afterwards related to him by marriage, and Malbone, were among his school-fellows. Ruth Gibbs, his cousin, destined to be his wife, was then a lovely little girl in the school.

Channing was not a brilliant pupil His teachers and schoolmates thought him a dunce He was very slow at his Latin. One day an assistant in his father's office said to him, "Come, Bill, they say you are a fool, but I'll soon teach you Latin." Soon the boy was enjoying Vergil, and he began to make great strides in mathematics. But from the first he was a thorough, not a superficial student. That was characteristic of him all his days.

It must have been a wonderful day for the boy when Washington came and dined with his father, about August 17, 1790 When Washington had made his eastern tour the year before he could not enter Rhode Island, for it was foreign territory, it not having adopted the Constitution In recognition of its entrance into the compact Washington made a special trip to this State in 1790 Under the same roof John Jay and other noted Federalists were entertained.

I have spoken of the influence upon young Channing of his father and mother and of Dr Stiles and Dr. Hopkins. At least one other helped to mould his youthful character, his grandfather. William Ellery

William Ellery, born in 1727, married early in life Ann Remington, of Cambridge, Massachusetts She looked well to the ways of her household, and he was a devoted husband British trade restrictions ruined his business prospects, and in 1770 he began to practise law. He was one of the leading spirits in the Sons of Liberty, who were so eager for separation from the Mother Country and Independence Rhode Island sent him with the venerable Stephen Hopkins to the Continental Congress Thus he became one of the signers of the Declaration of Independence. He was honest, fair-minded, and high-minded Channing, who reverenced his character, and who corresponded with him till his death in 1820 at the age of ninety-two, might have said of him as Marcus Aurelius said of his grandfather in the introduction to his "Meditations" "From my grandfather I learned good morals and the government of my temper."

One other influence played an important part in Channing's early life, communion with Nature He loved solitary walks and musings. Especially did he love to pace up and down Newport Beach The roar of the surf was "part of his life's unalterable good" "No spot on earth", he said, "has helped to form me so much as that beach There I lifted up my voice in praise amidst the tempest There, softened by beauty, I poured my thanksgiving and contrite confessions There, in reverential sympathy with the mighty power around me, I became conscious of power within. There struggling thoughts and emotions broke forth, as if moved to utterance by nature's eloquence of the winds and waves. There began a happiness surpassing all worldly pleasures, all gifts of fortune, the happiness of communing with the works of God."

One anecdote of Channing's childhood illustrates the serious impression made upon his heart and mind by what has been called "oratorical piety", by the preaching of dogma which is not taken in logical and literal reality His father, wishing to give him a drive, took him with him one day to hear a famous preacher who was holding forth in the neighborhood. Young William listened earnestly to the discourse With fervent utterance and glowing imagery the preacher described man's total depravity, his love of evil, his weakness, his need of divine grace, and the necessity of unceasing prayer. The world was painted in dark colors, a curse rested upon all. The boy felt sure that if this were true, everyone would give up his business and pleasure and start out to convert the unregenerate. As they left the church, his father said with emphasis to someone who had accosted him,— "Sound doctrine, Sir". "It is all true",— the boy thought. A cloud came over him. He was so depressed that he dared not speak to his father On the way his father began to whistle! Instead of calling the family together and telling them the awful news of man's doom, his father pulled off his boots, put his feet on the fender, and started to read his newspaper. Everything went on as usual. The lad was shocked at such apparent callousness "Could what he had heard be true? No! his father did not believe it; people did not believe it! It was not true!"

This was a rude shock to the boy's conscience. Henceforth he looked with distrust upon such theatrical preaching. He learned to measure the exact meaning of words and phrases. He detested public speaking that did not ring true. Sincerity he demanded above all things.

At the age of twelve Channing went to New London, Connecticut, to study with his uncle, the Rev. Henry Channing. That community was in the midst of one of New England's periodic revivals, and the young Channing seems to have been affected by it. His religious nature was awakened. During his visit he spent much time on a hill at Old Lyme, overlooking the sea. When on the one hundredth anniversary of his birth the church was built in Newport in his memory, the stone for it was brought from a quarry on that hill. From his New London studies he was suddenly called home by his father's death on September 21, 1792. After the funeral he went back to his uncle for a year, but he knew that on him and his elder brother would come in the future grave responsibilities. There was only a little property left by his father. But he left a good name, if not great riches, to his wife and children.

Channing entered Harvard College in the fall of 1794. Fourteen was then no uncommon entrance age. He did not live in the College Yard, but with his uncle, Chief Justice Dana, who had married his mother's sister. "He did not associate much with his classmates generally", we are told, but "drew about him a circle of choice and select friends". His intimate friends were Story, afterwards the great Judge and expounder of the Constitution; Joseph Tuckerman, whose name will always be associated with the ministry to the poor in Boston; and Jonathan Phillips, destined to be one of Boston's great citizens. In Channing's day there were one hundred and seventy-three students in the College. What a contrast to the Harvard of today, which has more than that number on the teaching staff!

In his recollections Channing's college life took on a gloomy tinge. "College", he says "was never in a worse state than when I entered it. Society was passing through a most critical stage. The French Revolution had diseased the imagination and unsettled the understanding of men everywhere   The tone of books and conversation was presumptuous and daring.   The tendency of all classes was to scepticism.   At such a moment the difficulties of education were necessarily multiplied. . . . The state of morals among the students was anything but good, but poverty, a dread of debt, and an almost instinctive shrinking from gross vice, to which natural timidity and religious principle contributed not a little, proved effectual safeguards."

Channing's college life covered the last two years of Washington's second administration and the first two of Adams's term.   The Federalists, who were English in their sympathies, were always in bitter controversy with the Jeffersonian-Republicans, who were friends of France. The overwhelming majority at Harvard was Federalist.   In 1798 Channing called his fellow-students together to protest against French aggression on the high seas and to offer to President Adams "the unwasted ardor and unimpaired energies of our youth to the service of our country".   All but three in the college signed it.   On his graduation in 1798 he was forbidden by the faculty to introduce current politics into his Commencement oration on "The Present Age"   He got around it by pausing in his oration and saying: "But that I am forbid, I could a tale unfold that would harrow up your souls"   Tremendous applause!

At Harvard he was a member of the Speaking Club, later called the Institute;   the Phi Beta Kappa;   the Adelphi, for those largely ministerially inclined;   the Hasty Pudding, started by his own class in 1795; the Porcellian, which was too "epicurean and convivial for his taste".

It was while Channing was reading Hutcheson, the English moralist, one day under the Cambridge willows, that there flashed into his mind that great idea which was to be "the fountain light of all his day, the master light of all his seeing",—the idea of the dignity of human nature.   It was his Damascus vision.   "He longed to die; as if heaven alone could give room for the exercise of such emotion"   The book awakened him spiritually.   He was also stirred by Adam Ferguson's "Essay on Civil Society".   Enthusiasm for social progress and the conception of moral perfection were awakened in his mind by Ferguson   Channing also dipped into Locke. Berkeley, Reid, Hume, and Priestley, Richard Price, also, loved by Benjamin Franklin, hated by Edmund Burke.   Channing happened to be in college during a Shakespearean revival, and felt its influence keenly.   When he came to choose his profession he first inclined towards the law.   But "the prevalence of infidelity" led him to examine the evidences for Christianity, "and then", he says, "I found for what I was made"

But he could not at once enter the ministry   He must work and earn some money, he must also make special preparation for his chosen profession.   Remember that this was before theological instruction had been differentiated from other college teaching.   The Divinity School of Harvard University did not come into being as a separate department until 1816   The custom then was for every college graduate who intended to enter the ministry to study with some older clergyman or to study by himself.   Channing, however, being without money, had to take up teaching for a while.   He went to Richmond as a tutor in the family of Mr David Meade Randolph, who had known him in Newport.   He taught Mr. Randolph's children and some others, a dozen in all   At his employer's table he met John Marshall and other great lights in Virginia social and political life.   The open-handed hospitality of the South he compared favorably with what he called "the selfish prudence of a Yankee".   But he said: "Could I only take from the Virginians their *sensuality* and their *slaves,* I should think them the greatest people in the world.   As it is, with a few great virtues they have innumerable vices."

As in New London, so in Richmond, the youth passed through a great spiritual awakening   The trouble was that it made him so morbidly introspective for the time that he strove to keep his body under by abusing it, eating insufficient food, sleeping on the floor in a cold room, wearing clothes that did not keep him warm.   He went to Richmond a vigorous youth, he left it a physical and nervous wreck. And all his life long he suffered from fearful headaches and nervous indigestion as a result of this unwise asceticism.

No monk of old ever tried any harder than he to exalt the spirit by punishing the body. In after life he realized the folly of this procedure. But it was too late to remedy the ills he had brought upon himself.

After nearly two years in Richmond he came back to Newport in July, 1800, the voyage being an exciting one, in a leaky coaling sloop with a drunken captain and crew Then his theological studies began in earnest. In a little office near the house his light, like Dr Hopkins's burned far into the night He spent much time at the Redwood Library, much at the Beach he loved. In 1802 he returned to Harvard as regent of the college, a sort of general proctor. He kept on his studies under the guidance of President Willard and Professor Tappan. In Cambridge he united with the First Church, over which was settled a moderate Calvinist, Dr Abiel Holmes, father of Oliver Wendell Holmes. His first sermon from the text, "Silver and gold have I none, but such as I have give I unto thee", delivered in several pulpits in and about Boston and in Hopkins's pulpit in Newport, attracted attention

He was called by two Boston parishes, the Brattle Street Church, where Dr. Thacher needed a colleague, and the Federal Street, a weaker and poorer church He accepted the Federal Street call on February 12, 1803, and was ordained and installed June 1, 1803. His uncle, Henry Channing of New London, gave the charge to the minister; his classmate, Joseph Tuckerman, gave him the right hand of fellowship; Dr Tappan preached the sermon The Federal Street Church was made up of the descendants of Scotch-Irish Presbyterians, who had founded it in 1729 In 1788 the Massachusetts State Convention met in it to ratify the Federal Constitution Hence the name of the street, Federal

Boston then had fewer inhabitants than Newport has now It was more like an old English market town than anything else "The social aspect," says Chadwick, "was that of the eighteenth century, and conservative at that Gentlemen of means wore colored coats and figured waistcoats, with knee-breeches and long white-topped boots, ruffled shirt-fronts and wristbands and stuffed white cravats, cocked hats (the more elderly) and wigs . . . . The

stately minuet was still the evening dance. In the summer
season Boston rivalled Newport as a place of Southern
resort, its anti-slavery atmosphere not yet sharpening its
east wind The big English dinner was the king-pin about
which the best society revolved This society was as exclusive of Jeffersonian Republicans as freezing water of animal
germs. A lady of the period said, 'I should as soon have
expected to see a cow in a drawing-room as a Jacobin'.

"Boston had, in 1803, little to show of that intellectual
life of which eventually it had so much. In fact, Channing.
Buckminster, and Norton were the prime movers of the new
regime. Few could speak French or read it. Madame de
Staël's 'L'Allemagne' (1814) was the first seed of German
studies, and its growth was slow. The Queen Anne men
reigned in literary taste. If Burns had been discovered, it
was probably by some miserable Jeffersonian. Wordsworth's first American reprint was in Philadelphia in 1802
Of creative ability there was none, except as Nathaniel
Bowditch's 'Practical Navigator' had set sail in 1800, and
Jedidiah Morse..had published his geography. The best
promise of Prescott and Bancroft and Motley and Parkman
and Fiske and Rhodes was the local work of Jeremy Bel-
knap, founder of the Massachusetts Historical Society, who
died in 1798. There were good lawyers like Dexter and Par-
sons; and Fisher Ames was magnified in the local atmosphere to the proportions of a Burke or a Bossuet. The sure
thing about Ames was that he was a political pessimist of
such sombre hue that his temper overhung the common consciousness of Boston like a leaden pall. In 1795 he feared
that he might outlive the government and the Constitution of
his country, and naturally his gloom had deepened with the
triumph of democratic principles. He complained that
even the Federalists did not appreciate as they should 'the
progress of licentiousness', a euphemism for the spread of
Jeffersonian opinions There were perhaps five hundred
who did so, and perhaps not.

"Fisher Ames's five hundred thorough-going pessimists
included, Mr Henry Adams thinks, nearly all the Massachusetts clergy In Boston and vicinity these clergymen were
nearly all Unitarians, the doctrines of the Trinity and the

more distinctive doctrines of Calvinism having for them no longer any attraction. Had Jefferson been aware of this, his fear and hate of the New England clergy would have been qualified in no slight degree, for his enthusiasm for religious liberality was even greater than for political. But he formed his ideas of them upon the clergy against whom he had contended in Virginia, men impervious to ideas, 'beasts at Ephesus', whose fangs had left their memories in his shrinking flesh. But what we are bound to consider is the effect which the political temper of the clergy had upon the expression of their theological opinions. Within a week of Channing's ordination, the Rev. Jedidiah Morse, of Charlestown, preached the Election Sermon, and he said, 'Let us guard against the insidious encroachments of *innovation*— that evil and beguiling spirit which is now stalking to and fro in the earth, seeking whom it may destroy'. Morse was Calvinistic, but his temper, a more important matter than his opinions, was that of the whole body of clergy of which Channing had now become a conscious part. Dr. Hedge has characterized the period immediately preceding Channing's settlement as 'the dryest in the history of the American pulpit'. The impression made by Channing's early preaching was enhanced immensely by its vivid contrast with the prevailing tone "

Channing began his ministry as a kind of combination of Calvinist and Hopkinsian, but after a few years his latent liberalism began to show itself For a century the Congregational churches of New England, more especially Massachusetts, had been, theologically, in a state of evolution. Rigid Calvinism, with its iron decrees, in many parishes gave way to milder Arminianism, with its emphasis on Divine Love and Grace. Many Arians, who read in their New Testaments that the Son was subordinate to the Father, began to doubt the co-equality of the Three Persons in the Godhead Later humanitarian conceptions of Jesus as the first-born of many brethren and not as absolute Deity, crept into the preaching of many pulpits. The process was so gradual and so quiet that not until 1815 did the Orthodox party awake to what was going on. Then came the Unitarian-Trinitarian controversy which split the Congregational churches wide open. As a result, the great majority of the ancient parishes of Massachusetts espoused the Unitarian side, preserving their historic continuity and corporate life without change of name or covenant. The First Church of the Pilgrims in Plymouth and the First Churches of the Puritans in Salem and Boston, adhered to the Liberal cause In many cases the Trinitarians felt obliged to go out and form new parishes, in order to retain the old doctrinal standards In some cases the Unitarians were forced out. The important point is that Channing and the Liberals in the Congregational churches had no intention of starting another sect. They desired to be known merely as Christians or Congregationalists The opprobrious name Unitarian was fastened on them by their opponents, the Calvinists, who gave no quarter and asked for none. But when it became a badge of reproach they wore it as a badge of honor, as the Wesleys did when at Oxford they were derisively called Methodists.

In his "Literary History of America" Professor Barrett Wendell says "The Unitarianism of New England, of course, was not unique either theologically or philosophically In its isolated home, however, it chanced to develop one feature which distinguishes its early career from similar phases of religious history elsewhere The astonishing personal purity and moral beauty of its leaders combined with their engaging theology to effect the rapid social conquest of the whole region about Boston King's Chapel and Harvard College passed into Unitarian hands. The same was true of nearly all the old Puritan churches .

"The general conquest of ecclesiastical strongholds by the Unitarians deeply affected the whole structure of Massachusetts society. Elsewhere in America, perhaps, and surely in England, Unitarianism has generally presented itself as dissenting dissent, and has consequently been exposed to the kind of social disfavor which aggressive radicalism is apt anywhere to involve. In the isolated capital of isolated New England, on the other hand, where two centuries had established such a rigid social system, the capture of the old churches meant the capture, too, of almost every social stronghold. In addition to its inherent charm,the pristine Unitarianism of Massachusetts was strengthened by all the force of fashion in a community where somewhat eccentric fashion has always had great weight. Whoever clung to the old faith did so at his social peril."

It is not my intention to go deeply into the controversy which made a divided fold of the Congregational communion. But I must call attention to some of the high-water marks in that raging storm. These were Channing's 1815 article on "The System of Exclusion and Denunciation in Religion", when he said, "Could the thunders and lightnings of excommunication have corrected the atmosphere of the church, not one pestilential vapor would have loaded it for ages", and the articles of 1819 and 1820 on "Objections to Unitarian Christianity Considered" and "The Moral Argument against Calvinism", in which he maintained that "Christianity contained no such doctrines [as those of Calvinism] Christianity was designed to manifest God in a character of perfect benevolence." He laid stress on "inward purity, heavenly-mindedness, love of Jesus Christ and God" In his Baltimore sermon of 1819, at the ordination of Jared Sparks, Channing dwelt on "the moral perfection of God, the oneness of his justice and mercy, his parental character, his freedom from those traits which constituted him a being whom we cannot love if we would, and whom we ought not to if we could". He rejected the idea that "Christ's suffering was a price to God to buy his mercy to mankind". In 1821 at the dedication of the Second Unitarian Church in New York he preached on "Unitarian Christianity most favorable to Piety", giving nine reasons why it is. "(1). It presents one object of supreme homage, and does not distract the mind with three persons having distinct qualities and relations. (2) It holds inviolate the spirituality of God, not giving him a material human frame (3) Its object of devotion is as simple as it is sublime. (4) It asserts the absolute and unbounded perfection of God's character. (5) It accords with nature, with the world around and within us (6) It introduces us to new and ever larger views of God (7) It assigns to Jesus his highest proper place—that of the greatest of the sons of God. (8) It meets the wants of sinful men (9) It is a rational religion."

In his Election Sermon of 1830 Channing said: "I call that mind free which jealously guards its intellectual rights and powers, which calls no man master, which does not content itself with a passive or hereditary faith, which opens itself to light whencesoever it may come, which receives new truth as an angel from heaven, which, whilst consulting others, inquires still more of the oracle within itself and uses instructions from abroad, not to supersede but to exalt and quicken its own energies"

Channing strongly opposed the War of 1812, considering it an unnecessary and iniquitous war. But in 1814, when it was expected that the British would land on our shores, he preached on the duty of manly self-defence And at the "solemn festival" of thanksgiving for the downfall of Napoleon he cried out in his sermon, "The oppressor is fallen and the world is free"; whereupon the congregation in King's Chapel burst into cheers. In 1816 his sermon on "War", before the Massachusetts Convention of Congregational Ministers, caused the formation of the Massachusetts Peace Society, but driving with a brother clergyman on this island one summer day he doubled up his tiny fist and cried, "There are times when a man must fight".

In 1822 Channing, who had then been happily married to his cousin, Ruth Gibbs, for eight years, went abroad with her for his health In Rome he received word that his older boy had died,—a terrible grief to him In England he met Coleridge, who saw in him "a philosopher in the double sense of the word", saying, "He has the love of wisdom and the wisdom of love" Of his visit to Wordsworth, when the two rode together in a cart, which must have been like Emerson's wagon hitched to a star, Channing wrote: "We talked so eagerly as often to interrupt one another, and as I descended into Grasmere near sunset, with the placid lake before me, and Wordsworth talking and reciting poetry with a poet's spirit by my side, I felt that the combination of circumstances was such as my highest hopes could never have anticipated" After a score of years Wordsworth remembered that Channing's one great evidence of the divine origin of Christianity was "that it contained nothing which rendered it unadapted to a progressive state of society, that it put no checks on the activity of the human mind, and did not compel it to tread always in a beaten path."

In 1823 Channing returned from Europe, and the next year Ezra Stiles Gannett, grandson of Ezra Stiles, was ordained as his colleague   This gave him more time for public work outside the pulpit, lectures and addresses and articles For the next eighteen years he was constantly speaking and writing on such topics as Slavery, War, Self-Culture, Elevation of the Laboring Classes, Temperance, Annexation of Texas (which he opposed, as he did slavery), the Duty of the Free States, West India Emancipation, Milton, Fenélon, and Napoleon—a wide range of subjects, to all of which he brought his clear spiritual vision and kindling moral earnestness   All his essays are sermons, as Emerson's essays are. They could not be anything else.

In his attitude toward the slavery question, Channing was between two fires   The radical abolitionists like Garrison thought him timid and time-serving because he did not endorse all their methods of propaganda   On the other hand, the gentlemen of property and standing in his own church were so incensed at his anti-slavery views that some of them refused to speak to him on the street, and some only coldly bowed.   There is no justification for the scathing attack on Channing as a moral reformer which you will find in Maria Weston Chapman's appendix to the Autobiography of Harriet Martineau.   Lydia Maria Child has done him full justice   Channing had to bear much, first from the followers of Garrison who could not understand why he was not in sympathy with everything they said and did, and secondly from the standing committee of his parish which refused the use of the vestry of the church for a memorial meeting to his friend, Dr Charles Follen, an Abolitionist

Channing happened to be in Newport when the Broadcloth Mob hauled Garrison through the streets of Boston, but the outrage inspired his pen   In his pamphlet on "Slavery" he said   "A man cannot be property in the sight of God and justice because he is a rational, immortal, moral being; because created in God's image, and therefore in the highest sense his child; because created to unfold Godlike faculties and to govern himself by a Divine law written on his heart and republished in God's Word." Here speaks the spirit of the man who, as a child, was strongly impressed by the faithfulness of the blacks he saw in his own household and in neighboring households. Among them was "Duchess" Quamino, a free black of royal appearance, the epitaph for whose tombstone was written by him.

In his application of Christ's teachings to social problems Channing was far in advance of his day, even of our day. In a period when dancing and the theatre were banned by the pious-minded he could conceive of a rational place for such recreations. He watched with interest such experiments as Brook Farm and the Hopedale Community. In his own time he was the centre of inspiration for such social reformers as Dorothea Dix and Joseph Tuckerman and Bronson Alcott. We are amazed in reading Channing to note how he anticipated in thought if not in act modern methods of dealing with poverty, intemperance, child labor, the stagnant life of the poor, industrial injustice. So great was his reverence for man that he cried out when told of the custom of flogging then in vogue in the navy. "What! strike a man!"

It was this awe in the presence of the Divine upspringing in the human that made Channing sympathize in spirit, though not in doctrine, with Theodore Parker, the gift of God to slave-ridden America, and that caused him to view without alarm the radical trend of the theology of the Transcendentalists, with whose vagaries, however, he had no patience.

Practically every year of his Boston ministry he went to Newport, or, rather, to Oakland Farm at Portsmouth, for a long summer holiday. Here, with his wife and children and relatives and congenial friends about him, he felt that his happiness, in spite of ill health and the attacks of his opponents, was perfect. He loved trees and flowers, the dawn and sunset. He said: "I sometimes think that I have a peculiar enjoyment of a fine atmosphere. It is to me a spiritual pleasure rather than physical, and seems to be not unworthy of our future existence." Again he wrote: "What a blessing such day as this is! So much a creature of the senses am I still, that I can find on such a morning that it is easier to hope in God, and to anticipate a boundless good for my race."

From his long retreats", says Chadwick, "he went back to

the city with a dewy freshness on his mind and with the salt
air reminiscent in the tang of many a bracing thought."

It was his custom every summer to preach to the farmers and fishermen in the Portsmouth Christian Church
Fashionable folk drove out to hear him on such occasions,
but he resented their coming. One day he began his sermon
in his low, thrilling voice, without preface or text, "This is a
beautiful world". You remember how the aged St. John
used to be brought, so runs tradition, into the Christian
assembly at Ephesus, that he might merely say to them all,
"Little children, love one another" That was Channing's
basic thought, "This is a beautiful world".

Sometimes he went into Newport and preached for Mr.
Brooks, whom he ordained in 1837, and at whose marriage he
officiated He took part with joy in the year 1836 in the
dedication as a Unitarian Congregational Church of the old
meeting-house on Mill Street, in which he had sat as a child
and listened to Dr. Hopkins and in which he had preached
his first sermon in Newport.

"One Sunday afternoon", Mr Brooks tells us, "when the
impatient horses of the fashionable hearers were pawing and
stamping in the street, Dr Channing, insisting upon the existence and nearness of evil from which we, too, needed deliverance, and of people's insensibility to it, exclaimed, 'They
are as indifferent to it as the very animals that stand waiting
for them at the church door!' "

It was at Mr Brooks's ordination that Dr Channing,
giving him the charge, said in thrilling tones, "My brother,
help men to see!" And that was what Charles Timothy
Brooks did in his long ministry of thirty-seven years in this
community He took the torch of truth from Channing's
hand and passed it on to us Fragrant be his memory!
Like Channing and their common Master, he was an Apostle
of Light.

On April 7, 1842, his sixty-second birthday, Channing
preached his last sermon in Federal Street Church. On August
1st, he delivered his great address at Lenox on the eighth anniversary of West India Emancipation, closing with these
words: "O come, thou kingdom of heaven, for which we daily
pray! Come Friend and Saviour of the race, who didst shed
thy blood on the cross to reconcile man to man and earth to

heaven! Come, Father Almighty, and crown with thine omnipotence the humble strivings of thy children, to subvert oppression and wrong, to spread light and freedom and peace and joy, the truth and spirit of Thy Son, through the whole earth!"

On the 2d of October, 1842, he lay dying in an inn at Bennington, Vermont, and as he looked out on the lovely Green Mountains his last words were: "I have received many messages from the spirit." He passed onward and upward looking eastward, waiting for the dawn of another morrow.

When the sacred dust was carried to Boston, the bells of the Roman Catholic Cathedral were tolled with all the rest in the city, for when the saintly Bishop Cheverus died had not Channing honored his memory? And when Dean Stanley visited Boston he asked Phillips Brooks to take him first of all to Channing's grave in Mount Auburn

In his great work, "God in History", the learned and devout Baron Bunsen called Channing a "grand Christian saint and man of God—a prophet of the Christian consciousness regarding the future and destined to exert an increasing influence. If such a man be not a prophet of God's presence in humanity, I know of none such."

In France, M. Laboulaye, of the Institute, translator of Channing's works into French (and into how many languages they have been translated!) has said· "If Channing were but one sectary more in the religious Babel, I should not have called attention to him, but he was a good man who, all his life, consumed by one sentiment and idea, sought truth and justice with all the forces of his intellect and loved God and man with all the strength of his heart"

M. Lavolée, a Roman Catholic scholar, whose book, "Channing: Sa Vie et Sa Doctrine", was crowned by the Academy of Moral and Political Sciences, compares him with Fenélon, saying: "Both have vowed to Jesus a love equally lively and profound; but, while the one adores and prays, the other contemplates and reveres."

And the Quaker poet, Whittier, cries:—

> "In vain shall Rome her portals bar,
> And shut from him her saintly prize,
> Whom in the world's great calendar
> All men shall canonize."

REV. DR. EZRA STILES

A Paper read before the Newport Historical Society
July 10th, 1917

By

REV. RODERICK TERRY, D.D.

EZRA STILES

It was the golden age of Newport's history, when the afterglow of the brilliant light shed upon its literary life by the presence of Bishop Berkeley culminated in the Philosophical Association whose weekly meetings furnished the thought which brought about the existence of the Redwood Library At this time Newport was among the leading cities of the colonies in intellectual activities, and seems to have deserved that name which was given to it, "The Athens of America." At that period of our history we ranked among the first mercantile centers, the sails of Newport ships whitening every known sea, while successful merchants built their beautiful houses and still more beautiful gardens which became noted throughout the world The hearts of men were then thrilled with the thought of possible freedom from the persecutions and enthralment of England, and Newport took its place also in the forefront of this patriotic movement

During these golden years, our city drew to itself many men of renown—statesmen, soldiers, scholars and artists—but none who brought to its life richer gifts of learning and piety than did Ezra Stiles. He stands prominently forth as a leader in the intellectual life of the city, as one of the most influential among its religious teachers, and as a patriot whose clarion voice called out for freedom, and roused the willing minds of his neighbors to serious thinking of liberty, and to overt acts of so-called rebellion.

Ezra Stiles was born in North Haven, Connecticut, December 10, 1727, his father being the pastor of the Congregational Church of that village. The Stiles ancestry, both in

---

The references in this paper are taken from "The Life of Ezra Stiles", by his son-in-law Abiel Holmes, printed in Boston 1798, and "The Literary Diary of Ezra Stiles", three volumes, New York, 1901; and "Itineraries and Correspondence of Ezra Stiles", New Haven, 1916. These last two works are edited by Francis Bowditch Dexter, Litt. D., who has kindly given permission for the use of these quotations

this country and in England, were of the strong Puritan Dissenter type, all being Congregationalists of that sturdy and intellectual quality which belonged to so many of the earlier residents of New England.

His mother was Keziah Taylor, whose father, the Rev. Edward Taylor of Westfield, Massachusetts, had fled from the persecutions which his family and friends had suffered through being Dissenters, and had come to America in 1668 He was of the same intellectual and religious stuff as were the Stiles. There was, however, in the mother's ancestry a strain of nobility and of attachment to the Church of England, which came from her great-grandmother, Mabel Harleykendon, who, a descendant of kings and of the English nobility, had come to this country and had married a governor of Connecticut. With a knowledge of this commingling of the staunch blood of the Dissenter with the more gentle blood of the nobility of England, we are able to understand some of the characteristics which will later appear in Ezra Stiles.

We are told that in Dr. Stiles' infancy his constitution was so feeble that it was long doubted whether he would survive the age of childhood, and only by exercising the greatest care by regulation of his diet and daily exercise in the open air, was he able not only to survive that period, but to perform during all the years of his life constant and unwearied labors.

His intellectual activity was noticeable even from his youth At the age of twelve he was prepared to enter college, but delayed matriculating until his fifteenth year, when in 1742 he became an undergraduate at Yale. For thirteen years he lived in that University town, remaining there after his graduation pursuing independent studies, and acting as a tutor in the college.

During these years he passed through curious and interesting phases in his religious experience, and not until the end of this period was he thoroughly confirmed in his belief. A man of keen intellectual discernment, and ever seeking for new light upon all matters scientific, literary and theological, it was impossible for him to separate his intellectual processes from his religious belief, and with the utmost deliberation and the broadest examination of all facts bearing on each particular question, he decided in regard to his faith, not according to that he had imbibed in his youth, nor according to that which was held by his fellow religionists, but every problem was thoroughly studied and his conclusions were firmly established In no case was the instruction of the apostle more fully carried out in regard to these matters of belief, "let every man be fully persuaded in his own mind "

We are all well aware of the character of the faith of the Congregational churches throughout New England at the time of his birth Like so many of his contemporaries he grew up in that belief which we know as Orthodox Calvinism, and probably had little more idea of criticising the prevailing faith than had any of his neighbors; but it must have been pretty early in his life that he began to be troubled in regard to his theological views, for he declares that when he reached the age of nineteen imagining himself to have *experienced and ended the period of doubt,* he united with the Congregational Church of which his father was the Pastor But this period of doubt was not ended, and his mind soon again became troubled He came into contact with the Deists, a set of thinkers at that time of very considerable influence in New England, who, while they professed faith in God, were yet uncertain regarding any authority to be placed upon the sacred Scriptures It was a phase of the never-ending conflict between reason and childlike faith; and naturally a man with such a mind as Dr. Stiles at first desired to place his whole confidence in reason, attempting to support himself in his inherited beliefs by the study of the recommended theologians. At length he thought himself satisfied in his own mind, and in 1749 was licensed to preach the Gospel. But he exercised the right very sparingly, and indeed soon gave up preaching altogether, until his faith should have been more firmly established. As he himself expresses it:

* "My doubt increasing until 1752, I determined to lay aside preaching, and actually adopted the study of the law, and took the

*Holmes, p 36

attorney's oath in 1753 But at the same time I most assiduously applied to the study of the evidences of Revelation, read through the Bible with the greatest criticism and examination, compared its several parts with each other, and the whole with profane history, and so far emphasized and felt the prevalence of evidence in its favor that by 1754 I had acquired a strong and prevailing preponderency to the belief of Revelation . . .   I could not see anything against the fulfillment of prophesy and the Christian miracle, but what would equally overturn the credit of all history I made these researches only for the sake of my personal religion, and that I might be at peace with God

Having acquired this satisfaction concerning Revelation. I next in 1754 availed myself of journeys to Boston, New York and Philadelphia, and determined by history to inform myself of all the sects in the Christian world This summer at Newport I went to the Quakers' Meeting, at Boston to the Congregational and Episcopal Churches, at New York the Episcopal and Dutch Calvinist, at Philadelphia to the Quakers, the Roman Catholics and others, with a fair and unprejudiced mind, and I was soon confirmed in that form of worship in which I had been educated, and which I was convinced was the nearest the apostolic form and Scriptural model.

"In 1755, my doubts having given way, I could honestly devote myself to the service of the Great Immanuel Just as I had emerged from Deism, or rather the darkness of skepticism, it pleased the Head of the Church to open the door at Newport "

How thoroughly this religious experience is in sympathy with his strong intellectual mind' which was always looking for information, never satisfied until he had learned all that could be learned, and from it made his clear deductions.

Yet was he no worshipper of his own intellect; he had respect for higher authority.

> "I begin to be confirmed in this," he writes, "that there is not a single doctrine or point of pure revelation whose rationale is revealed and explained so clearly that taking away the support of *certain* revelation, it would stand on the internal evidence, or be supported of itself alone upon the reasonings adduced. We can go but little further than to show that a doctrine is not inconsistent with reason. I would rather deduce the reasonableness of a doctrine from its being revealed by God than infer its being revealed from the supposed reason we may perceive in it. My wish, therefore, is that the truths of our holy religion be no longer mutilated and dishonored by human reasonings upon them, but be thought and delivered more didactically and directly from the Bible, with a 'Thus saith the Lord.'"

As we might expect, his faith, built upon such a foundation, was firm and unchangeable during the remainder of his life. No longer influenced by inherited ideas, by no means of that class of indolent mentalities who take the easiest course, he was one who fulfilled the Biblical instruction to "Prove all things, and hold fast that which is good."

It is not to be wondered at, however, that such a course of theological education should have brought down upon him the criticism and misunderstanding of his neighbors. The mere fact that, as he said, he visited all the different churches with an open mind to their good points, that if he found any that seemed to him preferable to the one in which he had been educated he might unite himself with it, naturally resulted in misunderstanding upon the part of his fellow-Congregationalists, as well as those of other faiths

> * "I have differed," he writes, "from most of my brethren in New England in a too great

---

*Literary Diary, January 19, 1777

extent of charity, judged more of different communions true children of God than they did. And when I first set out in life I had a much better opinion of mankind and the different sects as to sincerity and virtue than I now have. I never was particular and exclusive enough for cordial and close union with any sect, even my own . . my soul unites most sincerely with the whole body of the Mystical Church, with all that in every nation fear God and love our Lord Jesus Christ. . . . There is a preference of systems, but no perfect one on earth. I expect no great felicity from fellowship and open communication with mankind But intend to become more and more the recluse, waiting for the rest of Paradise, where I foresee my soul will unite with affection and acquiescence in eternal universal harmony."

These are very startling phrases for a New England Congregationalist in the eighteenth century, and proved that had Dr. Stiles lived at a later period, he would have shared, indeed probably, have led in the broadening views which have distinguished the Protestant Church in the last fifty years.

Naturally perhaps some of the other denominations misunderstood this breadth of feeling and desire to see the good in everything, and from the fact that he attended their services, were led to believe that he might become one of them ,for Dr Stiles writes,

*"In January of the year 1755 I had a formal invitation from the Episcopal Church in Stratford, Connecticut, to conform and succeed (as rector) Dr Johnson, lately appointed President of Kings College, now Columbia College, New York, and before that, in October, 1752, I sustained a vigorous application to take orders and become a minister in the Episcopal Church

*Holmes, p. 40

in Newport, then offering a living of two hundred pounds sterling. I thank God that I was not
disposed to profess a mode of religion which I
did not believe for the sake of the living "

Through Dr. Stiles' mature years he remained satisfied
with the faith of his youth. As he himself often said, the
more he investigated other religions, the more satisfied he
was that the doctrines of his church were the nearest to
those prompted by the Scriptures   He never regretted that
his religious home was in the Congregational Church.

This incomplete picture of his religious thinking may
well come to an end by these words regarding his personal
character, written by his son-in-law

* "Piety like a golden chain has served at
once to give a connection and ornament to the
work, which the assemblage of genius, learning, and the most refined morality could never
have furnished. Were any one of his Christian
graces to be discriminated, it should, perhaps,
be his humility, a virtue seldom attached to
great intellectual talent and to high stations,
but which confer the truest dignity on both."
"How absolutely contemptible," writes Stiles
in his Diary, "is a man glorying in some little
eminency among his fellow worms."

Not less striking than his theological liberality, and
perhaps more noticeable, was his intellectual acquisitive-
ness. His mind, like a great sponge, absorbed every item
of knowledge which came within its reach; into the natural
sciences, into linguistic studies, into the law, he plunged
deeply and continuously, almost to the same extent that he
buried himself in theological thought

In scientific studies he was ever thirsting after knowledge. When Benjamin Franklin in 1749 sent to Yale
College the first electrical machine to come into New England, Ezra Stiles was the one of all the people studying in
New Haven to apply himself to an examination and mastery

*Holmes, p 377

of this new phenomenon of nature and thus to make the first electrical experiments in New England. A correspondence with Franklin began at that time, which continued during the rest of his life.

He was ever seeking for knowledge from every possible source. He writes to Mr. Bruce, a celebrated traveler of England, to solicit more explicit information on parts of Abyssinian geography and history; to Sir William Jones, President of the Asiatic Society, expressing great inclination to see a copy of the Patriarchal Ages and Chronology, as found in the Pentateuchs of Cochin. Indeed from that study of his on Clarke street there went out questions to all parts of the world, to England, France, Greece, the Holy Land and Astrachan

His name was known so favorably abroad that the University of Edinburgh conferred upon him the degree of LL D., and naturally the colleges of his own country, Princeton, Dartmouth and Yale, and many learned societies continually honored him

His deep interest in scientific studies was keen. In regard to astronomy his Diary is replete with notes referring to the movements of the Heavenly bodies. His description and notes upon the transit of Venus in 1765, and the transit of Mercury, compose a quarto volume He was interested in geography, and for a long time puzzled in regard to the question as to whether Asia and America made one continent, but in 1769 he writes to his satisfaction,

* "It is now known that Asia is separated
from America by water, as certainly appears
from the Baron Dulfeldt's voyage around the
north of Europe into the Pacific Ocean."

But not alone in the matter of science was his eagerness for information noticeable. He had a thorough knowledge, we are told, of the Hebrew, Greek and Latin languages, and very few if any on this side of the Atlantic had made so great progress in a knowledge of Samaritan, Chaldee, Syriac and Arabic. On the Persian and Coptic he bestowed some

*Holmes, p 76

attention The French he wrote with facility. At the age of twenty-three he pronounced in honor of Governor Law the first of a large number of Latin orations, which were called forth upon every occasion of importance, and in the giving of which he was an adept. One in which we may be particularly interested was at the Commencement of Yale College in 1753, when he pronounced a Latin oration in memory of Bishop Berkeley, who died in January of that year

It is a satisfaction for some of us to find that he was a strong upholder of the study of the classics, and entered into discussion with Rev. Mr Rousmeyer, the Moravian minister at Newport, upon the question of the relative merits of the ancient and modern writers, for his friend desired to substitute modern Christian for ancient pagan authors Dr. Stiles' judgment on this is as follows

> *"There can be but one objection, that the Greek of Homer, Xenophon and Thucydides, and the Latin of the authors of the Augustan Age must be purer than the moderns, the Hebrew of Moses and Isaiah purer than that of the later Jews, so that I rather incline to the ancients—banishing Horace, Juvenal and the unchaste tribes, and making choice of the best— Cicero, Justin, Tacitus, Virgil for Latin, Homer, Xenophon, Plato and Dionysius among the Greeks I think cannot be excelled for purity of language"

Professor Meigs writes of him:

> †"He was familiarly acquainted with the jurisprudence and civil politics both of ancient and modern nations, the treasures of ancient history were made his own by diligent investigation, facilitated by his thorough acquaintance with languages, and of modern history he possessed an exact knowledge. His historical information has seldom been equalled Theology,

---

*Diary, April 2, 1771

†Holmes, p 354

however, was his most favorite study. To perfect himself in this was the ultimate aim and
object to which his vast and various scientific
attainments were directed and devoted. I have
known no man to express so sublime and mag-
nificent conceptions of the majesty of God as
exhibited in the works of Christ."

It appears strange that so few books were published by
such a learned man, and we must conclude that in regard
to each study he considered himself as one always "pressing
toward the mark" of satisfactory knowledge upon any subject, and never as "having attained" He had, however, in
mind the issuing of important works, for in 1762 he writes,

* "This day I first conceived the thoughts
of writing the history of the world, which has
never been well written according to the
genius and dignity of history. True and faithful narratives are as necessary to history as
good books to a library A roomful of books
thrown together in a confused, huge heap is no
library. The same of history, especially of the
world There is a purity, grandeur and dignity and enlargement and comprehension in
true, genuine history; of an empire, which
none ever reached but Livy,—of the world,
which was never yet reached. Voluminous
writing is not necessary to history The history
of the world may be contained completely in
one quarto volume, especially of such a small
world as this."

And from a letter written to him by Thomes Hutchinson
of Boston in 1764, we learn that he had the intention of
writing a history of this country. Neither of these plans
came to fruition, and the result of his intellectual labors as
preserved by the press are a large number of Sermons and
Addresses, and a few small volumes,—"The History of the
Judges (Regicides)" in 1796, also it is said an "Account of

*Itinerary, p. 51

the Settlement of Bristol, Rhode Island," in 1785, and Hammett in his "Bibliography of Newport" speaks of a book called "The Memoirs of Block Island or Manisses," written in 1762. "The above title," he adds, "is taken from the collections of the Massachusetts Historical Society. The book itself is not in their library, nor is there any mention of it in the manuscripts of Dr Stiles in Yale College Library." It would be interesting to know what authority the Massachusetts Historical Society had for mentioning such a supposed book.

The four volumes, three of Selections from Dr. Stiles' remarkable Literary Diary, and one from his Itinerary, so often referred to in this article, are mines of information in regard to the events of his time and his own investigations. Nothing escaped him He records natural phenomena most minutely. Being one of the few fortunate individuals at that time possessed of a thermometer, he records patiently day by day its figures. Distinguished strangers passing through Newport are mentioned by him On one occasion, as an astonishing fact, a priest of the Church of Rome visits the city on his travels, and of course this searcher after knowledge must have interviews with him. He studies the landscape, the lives of the birds, the actions of the tides In one of his walks he makes an interesting discovery, which he thus records in his Itinerary:

* "June 22, 1767.
1728 BELIEVE
  10 IN
  21 CHRIST
  &   LIVE IN NO SIN.

"This is an inscription which I took off a rock five and one-half feet long, two and one-half feet widest, on the shore at Brenton's Point, a little north of the river, and at the southwest corner of Rhode Island, five miles southwest of Newport. It is supposed to have been put on by Rev. Nathaniel Clapp. Two

*Itinerary, p 230

weeks later I viewed a stone at Price's Cove
The stone, light grey and hard, the inscription
'8 21 1728   GOD PRESERVE ALL MAN-
KIND' is daily trodden upon by the passing
fishermen.   The letters are done in the same
manner as those at the point about a mile westward   I suppose the 10 and 21 under 1728
denote 21st day of 10th month, or October 21,
1728.   Mr Clapp died in Newport 1745, having
labored in the ministry from 1695, or fifty years.

"On another stone is a number of seeming
incisions of the Wedge or Runic kind, but evidently the work of nature only"

In conjunction with Dr Samuel Hopkins he issued a
Manifesto against slavery, in connection with which it is
interesting to note this item in his Diary, dated February
26, 1775

"I propounded my negro servant Newport to be admitted into full communion in the church"

This man was bought for Dr. Stiles at Cape Mount on
the coast of Guinea in 1757, when supposed to be about
eleven years of age, in exchange for a hogshead of whiskey

We have but little information regarding the appear-
ence of Dr. Stiles, the following description which was made
about the time that he came to Newport being all that
seems to have been preserved   It was given by his son-in-
law.

* "A man of low stature, of a very delicate
structure, and of a well proportioned form,
whose eyes were of a dark grey color, and in a
moment of concentration singularly penetrating,   his voice was clear and energetic, his
countenance, especially in conversation ex-
pressive of mildness and benignity, but if occasion required it, becoming the index of majesty
and authority."

The first acquaintance Dr. Stiles had with Newport was
in 1754, in the course of a journey as far east as Boston.   It

*Holmes, p 349

is probable that during this visit he preached in one of the churches here, and we know that the next year, 1755, he went again to Newport in response to an invitation to preach in the Second Congregational Church, and in the following month, received a unanimous call to become the minister of that church

From what has been said of his religious experience, we may well understand the truth of his statement that this call somewhat embarrassed him, as he had determined to continue in the practice of the law; and he returned to New Haven resolved not to accept the invitation   But he writes,

> "At length, partly my friends. especially my father's inclination, partly an agreeable town and the Redwood Library, partly the voice of Providence in the unanimity of the people, partly my love of preaching and prospect of more leisure for pursuing study than I could expect in the law induced me to yield, and I gave an affirmative answer to the church and society."

At the College Commencement in September, he resigned his tutorship, after having filled that office six years and a half

On October 22 of this year, 1755, he was ordained the pastor of the Second Congregational Church, when his father, now venerable in years, preached the sermon upon the text, "Thou, therefore, my son, be strong in the grace which is in Christ Jesus." An interesting evidence of his power as a preacher and of his parental affection was contained in this discourse, and the counsel of the father was received by the son with filial reverence, and seems to have had a considerable influence upon his pastoral character

Dr. Stiles' personal feelings in connection with this important event in his life he thus describes in a letter to the Reverend Mr Hopkins of Hadley, formerly a fellow-tutor at Yale College.

---

*Holmes, p. 29

* "Last week I was ordained an instructor
of mankind in the Christian religion, but, alas,
who knows whether he shall teach men right or
wrong. Many have labored through life as
Christian ministers in recommending and in-
culcating errors, and how know I but I, fond as
others of my own imaginations, foolishly as
others apprehending them momentous principles, may spend also my life to little purpose
'Operose nihil agendo' (in laboriously doing
nothing). But Heaven knows I seek light. I
would gladly be informed on the genuine intentions of the Great Creator concerning man
Heaven preserve me from mistakes, and lead
me to a just, rational and thorough understanding of Christian truth."

It must have struck your notice that the church to
which Dr. Stiles was called was the Second Congregational Church, which naturally gives rise to the thought as
to why there should have been two. It came about in the
following manner.

At the first forming of the town of Newport, the Baptist
Church was organized, and most, if not all of the settlers,
having become dissatisfied with the Congregational spirit in
Boston, allied themselves with the Baptist Church, and
when the Massachusetts Congregational brethren, concerned about their religious condition, sent deputations here
to remonstrate, they generally had to return home disheart-
ened by failure. Cotton Mather in his "Magnalia" reports
this ill success thus,

"All the ministers which the Massachusetts
Colony sent with admonitions after them could
reclaim very few of them, and when the ministers of this province have several times at their
own united expenses employed certain ministers of the Gospel to make a chargeless tender
of preaching the word among them, this charitable offer of the ministers has been refused"

*Holmes, p. 64

But after that generation had passed to their graves, another and more successful effort was made by the Congregationalists of Boston, who sent one of their number to locate in Newport, and provided in large part for his support.

Nathaniel Clap was born in Dorchester, Massachusetts, in 1668, and graduated from Harvard College in 1690 He came here in 1695, and remained until his death fifty years later, in 1745. To him belongs the credit of having introduced Congregationalism to Newport His language regarding this enterprise is as follows:

> "About evangelizing the paganizing and perishing plantations bordering upon the Massachusetts province there had been anxious consultations, with supplications to the Lord. Finally in the year 1695, a number of people who were at least willing to keep together, invited one to come and preach here the following winter, after which they urged him to abide from time to time, until more than a score of years had rolled away."

At that time there had already been gathered in Newport several congregations of Baptists, companies of Quakers, Episcopalians, Seekers, as they were called, and probably others, so that this plantation could hardly have been called paganizing and perishing. The first services were held in the Colony House, which antedated the present State House, and is still standing It is on the west side of Prison street, which runs from the Parade to the back of the present jail, and is number 12

These facts and some of the following I have obtained from the "History of Congregationalism in Newport," written in 1896 by the Rev. R. W. Wallace, then pastor of the United Congregational Church.

He continues,

> "A law soon afterwards was passed, forbidding the use of the (Colony) building for religious purposes, and Mr. Clapp and his little

congregation were left without a place in which
to worship But this was an emergency which
they had the courage and the faith to meet,
and in 1696, a small church edifice was erected
on Tanner street, now West Broadway. near
Green Lane, which is now Tilden Avenue. This
was then an important residential section
Peterson says that the settlement of Newport
began in what is known as Tanner Street. and
extended through to Marlboro Street. After
years of faithful preparatory labor, the time
for the organizing of a religious body arrived,
and on the 3rd of November, 1720. an ecclesiastical council was held to form the church, and
to ordain and install its pastor The first celebration of the Lord's Supper was on October 1,
1721, when fifty-eight persons partook of the
Sacrament But Mr Clapp who, even according
to George Whitfield 'abounds in good works,
he gives all he has away, and is wonderfully
tender of little children,' had certain very peculiar views with reference to church discipline, and soon surprised everybody by a
positive refusal to administer the Lord's Supper
to the church, and also to baptize the child of
one of his church members. His reasons were,
so far as we can understand them, that in his
judgment his church members were not Christian enough to engage in so holy an act as
breaking bread in remembrance of Christ. and
in the case of the brother who was refused
baptism for his child, the pastor thought he
was not possessed of a piety deep enough to
consecrate his child to God."

Naturally trouble immediately began and misunder-
standings came from this austerity of Mr Clap, the
result of his Puritan training. In April, 1728. an ecclesiastical council was convened, which decided unfavorably in
regard to Mr. Clap's actions As he refused to recognize the

authority of the council, about one-half of the congregation withdrew, and April 11, 1728, organized the Second Congregational Church of Newport, selecting as its pastor the Rev John Adams

This Second Church obtained the use of the Tanner Street building, and Mr Clap and his adherents met for worship in the parsonage on the northeast corner of Church and Division Streets. In 1735 the Second Church erected a commodious meeting house on Clarke Street, which was the building in which Ezra Stiles preached during all of his ministry in Newport, and which is now, after many alterations, occupied by the Second Baptist congregation Later, the First Church, under Mr Clap's pastorate, built, in 1729, the church on Mill Street above Spring, which has lately been used by an auctioneer

We may look forward a little in the history of Congregationalism to express our gratification that these two churches eventually became one again, on the 4th of June, 1833, under the title of the United Congregational Church of Newport, which it still bears

For over twenty years the life of Dr Stiles was closely associated with all the activities and interests, intellectual and religious, of the city of Newport. It is impossible to speak of him simply as a preacher or pastor and not do justice also to the influence which he exerted upon the history of the town, and to the importance which the coming into this city and remaining here of such an active, intellectual mind was to the life of the community

His work here can be judged both from his own record of daily performance of duty, and perhaps with more fairness from expressed opinions of others His unusually extensive knowledge, and eager thirst to increase it, made him a marked man not only among the thoughtful of his own city, but wherever learning was appreciated in this country or other lands.

In a letter to the Rev. Dr. Welles, he expresses his feeling with reference to the work he had to do

' "I am stationed," he writes, "in a very difficult part of the Lord's vineyard, though I thank

*Holmes, p. 118

God with great tranquility and happiness in my
flock. A prince has not anything to bestow
which I should esteem of equal value with the
prayers of my brethren."

In his work as a pastor, he was one of the first, if not
the first, to inaugurate what are now known as prayer meetings In 1770, he having, as he himself informs us,

    * "Long had in contemplation to set up a
monthly meeting of the church by themselves
to pray and sing together, and to adapt a discourse to believers advancing and improving in
the religious life."

On January 14, 1770, he proposed the design. On the
evening of the next day, the church met at his house, and
attended the religious service. This elementary prayer
meeting was regularly maintained until the dispersion of
his church in 1775, and in a sermon preached after his
death by the Rev. Mr. Patten, his successor, it is stated that
"The memory of those meetings is still imprinted on the
hearts of a number who were interested in those pleasing
seasons of Christian communication".

From the numerous references in his Diary, and in the
enumeration of his pastoral calls, we may well perceive
that he made himself a familiar figure in all the households
of his church.

    † "As a pastor, he went regularly in and
out among his people The ease with which he
adapted himself to persons in different situa-
tions and of various characters and ages qualified him very much to promote the interests of
religion in his visits To the children and youth
he was affectionately and assiduously attentive. His memory will doubtless be extensively
preserved in the world, and it will long live in
this place. Scarcely a family nor an individual

---

*Holmes, p. 142
†Patten Funeral Sermon

here but has reason from some office of good
will to remember him   Not a tree nor a brook
nor a scene around us but has engaged his ob-
servation."

As a preacher, he seems to have been of uncommon
power   The Rev Dr Trumbull says of him,

> * "His early discourses were philosophical
> and moral, and at first he was not so much
> admired as a preacher as he was as a friend, a
> gentleman and scholar. But gradually becom-
> ing less a Newtonian and more a Christian, he
> became a serious, zealous and powerful preach-
> er of the truthes (sic) of the Gospel. . . He who
> is convinced that the religion of the Gospel is
> true, and who has experimentally found it to
> be the power of God to his own salvation, will
> explain its doctrines and inculcate its precepts
> with an energy, not easily imitated and never
> equaled, by one who has no such conviction of
> the truth, and who is a stranger to its sancti-
> fying influence .   .   Furnished with a
> rich treasure of learning, he made it auxiliary,
> as the subject required, to the elucidation of
> religious truth, but never displayed it in the
> pulpit with ostentation. Instead of aiming at
> excellence of speech or of philosophical discus-
> sion of religious subjects, he was a plain, prac-
> tical, pungent preacher of the Gospel of the
> grace of God." . . . . and Dr. Holmes adds
> † "Extensive as was his Catholicism, his
> discourses never countenanced prevailing
> errors, nor sanctioned the opinion that religious
> sentiments are indifferent   Averse to disputa-
> tion and scholastic subtleties in divinity, instead
> of discussing theological subjects controver-
> sially, he chose the easier method of refuting

*Holmes, p. 237
†Holmes, p. 237

error by maintaining truth   Hence his sermons were instructive and pathetic While to the learned they were acceptable and improving, to the ignorant they were intelligible and practically useful. Such was the attention of the lower classes of the community to his discourses, and such the success of his labors among them that he judged his talents better adapted to promote their improvement than that of the wise and great. He delighted, therefore, in preaching the Gospel to the poor."

His relation to the intellectual life of the community is noted in various addresses and Diaries He himself declares that one of the things which induced him to come here was the existence of the Redwood Library, one of the very few then in the country, and notable among them for its carefully selected books Upon his being called to Newport, he was made an honorary member of the Library But evidently his spirit was moved at the indifference with which the Library was treated at that time, and he soon became its librarian for years occupying that position, spending all his spare moments among its treasures, and as he himself informs us, frequently for days at a time being the only visitor to the building.

His relation with the beginnings of Brown University is most interesting His correspondence shows that as early as 1761 he was endeavoring to bring about the foundation of a college in Rhode Island. His hope was that the two bodies, Baptists and Congregationalists, should unite in such an effort. But soon he sadly writes: —

> * "The Baptists desert their junction with the Congregationalists. and engross all the power in the proposed Rhode Island College to themselves, after they had agreed to share the balances with us."

In regard to the charter which was published in the Providence Gazette for April 28, 1764, he writes,

---

*In a Diary belonging to Mrs Kate Garnett Wells, Sept. 20, 1763

"This charter was drafted by Mr William
Ellery, Jr, and myself before the Baptists
deserted the Congregationalists."

September 7, 1769. speaking of the Commencement of
the college at Warren, the college which later became Brown
University, he sends this letter "To the Chancellor, President, Fellows and Trustees of the College of Rhode Island
Gentlemen: You will please to accept my respectful ac-
knowledgments for the honor you have done me in electing
me one of the Fellows of the College I was too sincere a
friend to literature not to have taken part in the institution
at first upon my nomination in the charter, had I not been
prevented by reasons which a subsequent immediate election
could not remove, which reasons are still of so much weight
with me that I beg leave to decline the office to which you
have invited me "

January 3, 1770, he says, "Dr Eyres visited me this
morning, to discourse about the place of the Baptist College
He tells me that Providence has subscribed 3,090 pounds, of
which about 2.200 truly is conditional that the college edifice
be erected there   Dr Eyres said that the Newport
subscription was about nine thousand dollars, but said they
did not choose to mention the amount exactly, nor how much
conditionally.

"The case is this, Mr. Redwood and some others have
said they would give largely, in case it was here, but that
Providence by artifice and stratagem would in event get it
there, and yet would not subscribe, but will undoubtedly
give liberally So there is a real uncertainty."

"May 3, 1770. The Baptist College was last week, or
week before, voted to be removed to Providence "

With his fellow-ministers of Newport he seems to have
sustained always the pleasantest relations Even though he
may have differed from them in his opinions, he never
opposed them in his feelings, and always looked for the good
rather than the evil, rejoiced in points of agreement, and
made as little as possible of those of disagreement between
himself and others

An instance of this is very notable in what he himself

says of his relation to Mr Samuel Hopkins, whose coming to the city caused a number of their fellow-ministers in the Congregational Church considerable anxiety, as witness this letter to Dr Stiles from Rev Charles Chauncey.

* "Boston, November 14, 1769. I am sorry with my whole soul that Mr. Hopkins is like to settle at Newport. He is a troublesome, conceited, obstinate man He preached away almost his whole congregation at Barrington, and was the occasion of setting up the Church of England there He will preach away all his congregation at Newport or make them tenfold worse than they are at present. I wish his installment could be prevented "

But Dr. Stiles, recognizing what he believed to be the true Christian spirit of Dr Hopkins, welcomed him cordially as a brother minister, preached the sermon at his installation, and during all the time that they were together in the city, continued on terms of the greatest friendship and sympathy, although they could easily have found occasions for difference had they so desired.

One of the most interesting of his ministerial relations was that with the Jewish Rabbi. With his thirst for learning, Dr. Stiles instinctively selected that one among his fellow-ministers who could be of the most use in increasing his knowledge He attended the services of the Synagogue, and soon entered upon a friendly acquaintance He became the pupil of the Rabbi in the study of Hebrew, and of the history of the Jews.

Nor did he confine his Jewish studies to his relation with this resident of Newport, but corresponded in Hebrew with learned Jews in different parts of the world, in 1773 forming an acquaintance with Haijin Isaac Carigal, a learned Rabbi, a native of Hebron in the Holy Land A long correspondence was carried on between them.

In 1772 we find him writing a letter in Latin to the Rev. Dr. Busch, a Moravian minister in Astrakhan, near the

*Itinerary, p 450

Caspian Sea, the object of the letter being to make inquiries concerning the ten tribes of Jews who he was convinced by the prophets would yet be restored to the Holy Land. He believed that they must be somewhere existing distinctly among some nations of the earth.

* "Modern voyages and travels," he observes, "have laid open almost all countries and their inhabitants except the interior and most remote regions of Asia, which lay between the River Volga and the Sinensian Empire, or from the Caspian Sea toward the east, and from

India toward the north." That tract he most ardently wished might be thoroughly explored, in which he judged these tribes had hitherto remained concealed, and would hereafter be found; and in connection therewith he goes into a long history of the Jewish people and of the lost tribes. covering ten quarto pages, and adds,

"St. Thomas found a Hebrew damsel singing Hebrew psalms at the court of an Indian prince at Cranganor, near Cochin."

Not only did he attend the services in the Synagogue, but the Rabbi came upon at least one occasion to hear a sermon from Dr. Stiles on "The dispensations of God toward his chosen people, and the glory of the Messiah's Kingdom." It was the first sermon which the Jew had ever heard from a Christian preacher

In December 2, 1763, in his Diary he writes,

"In the afternoon was the dedication of the new Synagogue in this town It began by a handsome procession, in which were carried the Books of the Law, to be deposited in the ark Several portions of Scripture and of their service, with a prayer for the Royal family were read and finely sung by the priest and people. There were present many gentlemen and ladies The order and decorum, the harmony and solemnity of the music, together with a handsome assembly of people, in an edifice the most perfect of the temple kind, perhaps, in America, and splendidly illuminated, could not

*Holmes, p. 158

but raise in the mind a faint idea of the majesty and grandeur of the ancient Jewish worship mentioned in Scripture Dr. Isaac de Abraham Touro performed the service "

With his tendency to magnify points of agreement and to minimize points of disagreement between the different Christian bodies. we may well understand that he would frequently exert himself to bring about a better understanding

> ' "It has been a principle with me for thirty-five years past to walk and live in a decent, civil and respectful communication with all, although in some of our sentiments, in philosophy, religion and politics of diametrically opposite opinion; hence I can freely live and converse in civil friendship with Jews, Romanists, and all the sects of Protestants, and even with Deists. I am all along blamed by bigots for this liberality, though I think none impeach me of hypocrisy. I have my own judgment and do not conceal it "

He was always much interested in any possible union of different branches of the church. In 1759, when a young man, he brought the idea prominently forward in a letter. The next year he delivered before the Convention of Congregational Ministers of Rhode Island a discourse on Christian Union, in closing which he presents a fascinating picture of the condition when all the churches of New England shall be united into one.

This discourse, which was printed and became famous, roused considerable enthusiasm in the minds of a number of the Congregationalists of New England, but, alas, it was on too high a plane to suit most, and to a great degree failed of its object.

It was but a few years after his settlement in Newport that the question of the relation of the colonies to the mother country became acute, and no one took a more keen

*Holmes, p. 274

interest in the question, or more freely uttered his opinion than did Dr Stiles.

Some quotations from his Diary and letters may well be made His first criticisms upon the British policy that I have come across were written in the year 1759, in a letter to the Rev Dr Cumming of Edinburgh

> * "For us in New England," he writes, "to be harassed with even the most moderate Episcopacy, at least to have it imposed upon us, whose fathers fled hither for exilement, is perfectly cruel Free inquiry has made such progress as must inevitably pull down all ecclesiastical polities not founded in the sacred Scriptures. It would be more agreeable to this country if Presbyterians and Dissenters were not precluded from offices and employments in the gift of the Crown or the provincial governors "

In 1760, in a sermon preached on a day of Thanksgiving in consequence of the surrender of Montreal, he said,

> † "It is probable that in time there will be formed a provincial confederacy and a common council, standing on free provincial suffrage, and this may in time terminate in an imperial diet, where the imperial dominion will subsist as it ought, in election "

This is probably one of the earliest public statements of opinion regarding freedom in this country.

Liberty Day was celebrated in Newport March 18, 1769, the anniversary of the King's signing the repeal of the Stamp Act Of this anniversary celebration, Dr Stiles writes,

> ‡ "At dawn of day colors or a large flag was hoisted and displayed on the top of the tree

---

*Holmes, p. 76
†Idem, p 100
‡This and the following quotations are from the Diary

of liberty, and another on the mast of liberty at the Point at the same time. My bell began and continued ringing till sunrise. About nine o'clock A M the bell of the First Congregational Church began to ring, and rang an hour or two The Episcopal Church bell struck a few strokes and then stopped, the Episcopalians being averse to the celebration."

An interesting event occurred in the year 1770 It was customary for the clergymen of the Church of England to preach a sermon on the 30th of January in commemoration of the martyrdom, as they called it, of Charles I. The return of this day awakened Dr Stiles' indignation at the operations of the arbitrary king of England, and occasioned remarks worthy of an enlightened and ardent friend of liberty.

"This day," he writes, "if observed at all, should be celebrated as an anniversary of Thanksgiving, or memorial that one nation on earth had so much fortitude and public justice as to make a royal tyrant bow to the sovereignty of the people, to institute a judicial trial of a monarch, and sentence him to the punishment of the execution which he merited "

In regard to this sermon, his father-in-law, John Hubbard, of New Haven, wrote to him on the 15th of March,

"We have a story here that you disobliged the Episcopalians of Newport by a thirtieth of January sermon, and that you are like to be trounced for it, as their phrase is I hope the matter is much magnified. Please to let me know the event "

He again, however, on the 25th of July, writes,

"I thank you for your sermon, and am better acquainted with King Charles than ever I

was before, and were I to take my idea of a
martyr from him, should have as mean an
opinion of him as I have of some of the clergy."

Upon the death of George II and the accession of George
III in 1772, he had still more to say concerning the relation
of New England to the Crown, and in a letter to a Mrs Mc-
Cauley in England, he writes,

> * "Every step she (England) has taken for
> some years past, at least the general system of
> colony administration, has had as direct a ten-
> dency to accelerate events which she should
> keep at a distance as if projected from the
> deep laid policy of the Conclave. It is most
> firmly believed here that Providence intends a
> glorious empire in America "

And when one year later, 1773, the people of Rhode
Island burned the "Gaspee", Dr Stiles writes that he is "glad
to find that the sons of liberty in other colonies felt the attack
upon us, which is equally a stroke at universal American
liberty I have perfect confidence that the future millions
of America will emancipate themselves from foreign oppression."

> "June 30, 1774 Day of public fasting and
> prayer through the Colony of Rhode Island, by
> order of Assembly, on account of the threat-
> ening aspect of public affairs, the acts of Par-
> liament respecting America, and particularly
> on account of blocking up the port of Boston.
> I preached P. M. from Esther 4:3, 'There was
> great fasting and weeping and mourning, and
> many lay in sackcloth and in ashes,' to a very
> crowded assembly of all denominations. The
> day was kept in town very universally, not
> above half a dozen shops open in all the town.
> Mr. Bissett, the Church of England clergyman,
> took his text 'Fast not as the hypocrites,' and
> preached a high Tory sermon, inveighing by
> allusions against Boston and New England as a
> turbulent ungoverned people. The other con-

*Holmes, p 163

gregations in town were heartily in the cause of liberty. The Baptists seem to have little interest in the fast."

In 1774, November 5th, he records the parading the streets and burning in effigy of Lord North, Governor Hutchinson and General Gage Again in November 30th of that year, in speaking of the attempt of the French to dissuade from war, he adds,

"Great efforts are made by the ministry and their connections in America to detach the Baptists and Quakers throughout America from the Continental Union, and also the body of Episcopalians interspersed through the provinces north of Maryland, and with too much success. A languor prevails through these bodies. The defence and conservation of the public liberty stands on the union of the southern Episcopalians and the grand universal body of Congregationals and Presbyterians throughout the Continent. Perhaps the Baptists may open their eyes, but there is no hope of the Quakers."

April 25, 1775, he notes,

"Governor Ward yesterday wrote a letter to Messrs. Malbone, received today, advising the merchants to get their vessels to sea or out of New England with all speed, and recommending to the people of Newport to remove themselves and effects speedily, as there was certain danger of immediate seizure. This has thrown the town into great consternation and panic, and many are all day putting up their effects and preparing for removal. To heighten the terror, the men of war give out that if Newport takes part with Providence and New England, they will lay the town in ashes."

"October 8, 1775. Lord's Day. Preached on Lamentations I 4,5. 'The ways of Zion do mourn.' This is a most sorrowful Sabbath. In the afternoon there were about sixty-six persons below, and thirty-five in the galleries. My usual congregation three or four hundred We had a mournful meeting This morning we heard that Capt Wallace with his fleet fired on the town of Bristol last night. An inhuman wretch.

"October 9th. This day I removed one load of my books and furniture The carting of goods and removing of people continued all day yesterday, and yet continues. The infernal Wallace, with three men of war and other vessels, a fleet of perhaps eight sail, is firing away to the northward, and spreading, or aiming to spread, terror through the bay. It is judged that two-thirds of the inhabitants of this town are removed up the island.

"10th and 11th. Spirit of removal nearly ceasing, though some continue still removing These removals continued for several days By the nineteenth, three-quarters of the property and inhabitants had removed, most of the shops shut up, many houses shut, many more with only one or two persons to keep them; for the fortnight past as much as forty or fifty teams being daily employed, besides horse carts and boats.

"23rd October. This afternoon the remnant of my society met and judged it expedient to discontinue the public worship in my meeting house for the winter, considering the present evacuated and distressed and tumultuous state of the town They all recommended and consented to my removal to Bristol for present safety.

"November 2nd. Sent off a second load of goods, being part of my library and furniture

"December 11, 1776 The English officers are taking up houses for barracks, and among others have taken my house and meeting house which last it is said they intend to make an assembly room for balls, etc., after taking down the pews.

"December 26, 1776. I reviewed the town of Newport from memory and found the number of names of men with families now remaining in the whole town but 260. This confirms my judgment that two-thirds evacuated last year, in 1775. In the spring enumeration was made, 9200 souls in town. At six to a family, this would be fifteen hundred families, but truly there were eighteen hundred; now but 260. "

After the departure of the British he returned for a visit.

1780, May 21. Lord's Day. I preached to my dear flock in the rooms of my meeting house. Psalm 36.7 'How excellent is thy mercy, oh Lord, etc.' We had sixty-six benches, containing five or six persons each, making a congregation of three hundred and fifty persons, about two-thirds of which were my flock. I judge two-thirds of my congregation are returning to Newport The enemy had run up a chimney in the middle of the meeting house, and demolished all the pews and seats below and in the galleries, but they left the pulpit standing, though they destroyed the pulpit in the Presbyterian meeting house and in two Baptist meetings. My little zealous flock took down the chimney and cleared the meeting house, and then procured some benches and tables made for the King's troops' entertainments, and left behind, so that we attended Divine service very conveniently, though with a pleasure intermixed with tender grief.

"May 28. I preached and baptized William Ellery Channing, son of Hon William Channing, Esq., Attorney General of Rhode Island.

31 May. I took a melancholy farewell, and
left Newport on return for New Haven. About
three hundred dwelling houses I judge have
been destroyed in Newport The town is in
ruins. I rode over the Island, and found the
the beautiful rows of trees which lined the road,
with sundry coppices, groves and orchards cut
down and laid waste, but the natural beauties
of the place still remain, and I doubt not the
place will be rebuilt, and exceed its former
splendor."

And this is his Valedictory to Newport

"February 1, 1781. Very lamentable is the
state of religion in Newport, and particularly
that they will not attend public worship. One
occasion of this negligence is Brother Hopkins'
new divinity. He has preached his own congregation almost away, or into an indifference.
He has fifty or sixty families or more of his own
congregation in town, and might easily command a good assembly, if his preaching were as
acceptable as his moral character "

The pastorate of Dr Stiles in Newport had thus ended
in 1777, when the English took possession of the city. But
he was not to be left without a place of labor, for immediately a church in Providence sent him a most flattering call
to become its pastor, also a church in Taunton, and a little
later a prominent church in Portsmouth, New Hampshire.
The latter he finally accepted as a temporary labor

But very soon another and far more important position
was offered to him The first intimation came in a letter
from the Rev. Dr. Dana, of Wallingford, written on the 25th
of August, 1777.

* "Reverend and Dear Sir: There is reason
to believe that you may soon be invited to the
presidency of Yale College. I must entreat you
not to engage at Portsmouth for any length of
time, Providence is about to call you to a
higher trust."

---

*Diary, Sept 17, 1777

Another letter from Mr Whittlesey, Secretary of the Corporation of the College, September 13th, says,

> "I take the earliest opportunity to inform you that the corporation of our Almæ Matris this week made choice of you president of the College."

In regard to this Dr. Stiles writes, September 19, 1777.

> "My election to the presidency of Yale College is an unexpected and wonderful ordering of Divine Providence; not but that it has been talked of for years past, but I knew such reasons in the breasts of the Fellows, and I thought such were the sentiments of the assembly and the plurality of the pastors regarding my ideas in ecclesiastical polities and doctrinal systems of Divinity as that it was impossible I should be elected."

After several letters and visits from interested persons, he writes the corporation of the College on the 2nd of October,

> "I have thought it prudent and expedient to make a journey into Connecticut, and refer the matter to further consideration when I have had an interview with the corporation at their meeting next month"

That interview seems to have been satisfactory, and although he delayed his answer still again for a short time, he finally in August, 1778, wrote to the corporation accepting the presidency:* in the meantime having written to his Newport congregation and to many of his fellow-ministers for their opinion

The answer from the Newport congregation was a letter written January 30, 1778, by Mr. Benjamin Ellery, brother of William Ellery, the Signer.

> "Your little flock, deprived of part of their property, and scattered about the country, will

---

*Diary, February 12, 1778

not probably all of them ever collect again, and should the major part return to Newport, their circumstances will be so reduced that however willing they may be, it will not be in their power to afford you such a living as you deserve. I think, therefore, it will be best for you to accept the invitation to the presidency of Yale College, and if I could conceive the prayers of such a worm of the dust as I am to the Deity would be of any service to you, I would add them for your health, happiness and prosperity."

And the ministers to whom he referred the question had unanimously expressed their opinion that he should accept the position.

From 1778 to 1795 he held the office of president of Yale College, and there is need to say nothing here regarding the success of his administration. When he entered upon his labors the College was greatly reduced, in fact almost to the vanishing point, on account of the Revolution, but when he left it, it was a flourishing and influential institution

The extent and variety of his scholarship is evidenced from the fact that at different times when it became necessary, he filled the chairs of the professor in Mathematics, of Natural Philosophy and Astronomy, of Mental and Moral Philosophy, and of Ecclesiastical History; all, we are told, in a most satisfactory manner.

It may interest us to read in his Diary of March 15, 1781,

"I received of Mr Cook five hundred dollars in silver and gold, on account of rents of Dean Berkeley's Farm at Rhode Island, given to the College."

An opinion concerning him which is not without interest, however absurd, is expressed in the following extract of a letter from a foreigner in New Haven to his friend in New York, published in the New York Morning Post August 9, 1787

"On Thursday last the remains of Rev. Chauncey Whittlesey were interred. I attended this funeral, and at the brick meeting house, the place of interment, a fulsome farrago of nonsense, called here a funeral sermon, was preached forth by one of the crop-earred brethren, generally designated among the devout by the name of Pious Ezra This curious eulogium consisted of the most perfect adulation to the deceased, bordering even on impiety, the whole well larded with texts of Scripture, which were haled in by the head and shoulders at every other sentence, whether applicable or not. The sermon was upon the Parable of the Talents."

On the 8th of May, 1795, Dr. Stiles was seized with a bilious fever, and at four in the afternoon on the 12th, as his hopes of this world lessened and those of Heaven brightened, he took an affecting leave of his family, and expired at half after eight in the evening, in the sixty-ninth year of his age.

The funeral was held in the brick meeting house, which was crowded with the officers of the University, clergymen and other distinguished neighbors. Dr Dana preached the sermon on the text "In my Father's house are many mansions," in which he declares,

"The Ministry lament one who was their brightest ornament, the Church lament the truest friend of their religious order, the State and Nation lament the friend of their rights, the friends of Science and Liberty, of candor, of their country, and mankind, lament the loss to the world."

In a newspaper obituary published at that time, it is written,

"Of such an assemblage of varied excellence in a single person, the world has afforded but few examples."

CPSIA information can be obtained at www.ICGtesting.com
Printed in the USA
BVOW061128181112

305850BV00004B/65/P